The
Simultaneous
Policy

The Simultaneous Policy

An Insider's Guide to Saving Humanity and the Planet

John M Bunzl

New European Publications London

Published in the United Kingdom in 2001 by

New European Publications Limited
14-16 Carroun Road
London SW8 1JT, England

Editor   Dr. Aidan Rankin
Cover and page design   Lloyd Allen

British Library Cataloguing in Publication Data

ISBN   1-872410-15-4 hardback
        1-872410-20-0 paperback

Composed in Bembo & Perpetua
Printed and bound in Great Britain by Antony Rowe, Chippenham, Wiltshire.

Acknowledgements

I am grateful to many people who have taken the time to read and comment on drafts for this book. Among them I would like to mention Satish Kumar, James Robertson and Wolfgang Sachs. Their criticism has greatly helped in structuring the book and in rounding out its arguments more completely. I am also grateful to Ed Goertzen, Elias Davidsson, Bal Khela and Peter Merry who gave valuable advice in pointing out several aspects of the text likely to cause misunderstandings and, more particularly, to Dr. Aidan Rankin who pointed out that whilst the proposals put forward show a bias towards the political left, they can and do appeal right across the political spectrum. I am also grateful for the unstinting support received from Barbara Panvel, Peter Challen and Georges Drouet in helping to bring the theory of this book into practice. Last but not least, I also owe a debt of gratidude to my wife, Judy, and to my children, Alexandra, Thomas and Jacob for their support and forbearance at the unexpected distraction from my duties as a husband and father the Simultaneous Policy has caused.

The usual disclaimers apply.

Contents

Foreword

The fact that, when he came to office, President George W Bush firmly set his face against the United States implementing the Kyoto agreement on climate change lends weight to the main tenet of John Bunzl's argument – that destructive competition is the principal barrier to implementing measures to alleviate today's global problems. Commercial interests have so engineered control over political, economic, social and environmental programmes that only market-friendly policies are pursued regardless of whatever regime or party is in power. Not only does this market plutocracy destroy human value systems with disastrous environmental consequences but it also undermines the very roots of democracy.

Bunzl with his concept of Simultaneous Policy (SP) is offering a stimulus to go beyond the boundaries of conventional economic, diplomatic and sociological thinking. He argues that we need to make some fundamental changes to capitalist systems as they currently operate in the hope of closing the critical sustainability gap. The adoption of a Simultaneous Policy would eliminate the worst aspects of destructive competition from the economic system whilst promoting a recognition of the interdependence of each and all.

Whether or not the proposals in this book prove to be workable at the global multilateral level is not the main issue. By putting forward Simultaneous Policy John Bunzl offers a new slant on the globalisation versus localisation debate and the role of NGO's. He also provides a co-operative basis upon which world leaders can work out the practicalities as together they commit to undertake the implementation of simultaneous decision-taking whilst at the same time allowing scope for all the small scale, local grass roots initiatives. This duality of needs is part of our present human condition which requires addressing at both the micro and the macro levels.

The thinking aims at encouraging "a New Politics of co-operation and community which transcends both the divisions of conventional party politics and the dilemmas of maintaining international competitiveness".

Diana Schumacher,
Godstone, Surrey.
May 2001.

1. Introduction

Seeing the 50th D-Day anniversary celebrations just a few years ago and knowing my wife's uncle as one of its veterans, the sacrifice of soldiers on both sides was hard to imagine and even harder since the concept of sacrifice for one's country seems so totally remote and divorced from present realities. It occurred to me that the relationship between citizen and state had radically altered in the intervening years. For instead of waging war on one another, at least for the advanced and rich nations that together effectively police the world, there no longer appears to be any substantial threat to their continued existence nor to their dominance in the current world order. This sense of physical security enjoyed by their citizens, now even more real since the end of the Cold War, has engendered an atmosphere in which the immediate threat of war between them effectively no longer exists.

TWO WORLD PROBLEMS

For those of us living in rich northern countries, a stage has therefore been reached where, just as traditional threats seemingly recede into the mist, two relatively new threats have emerged to replace them. They have, of course, been ever-present but have never before come so sharply into focus. In this book, they are referred to as "our two world problems". They are, firstly, the threat posed by unsustainable consumption and pollution that characterise continued economic growth in a finite environment: a problem that could be summed up as humanity's need to achieve a type of livelihood compatible with a sustainable environment; in short, to achieve "Right Livelihood"[1]. Second, and not unconnected to the first, is the threat posed by the worsening poverty and dependency of the vast majority of the world's rapidly growing population. That some will be more fortunate than others, or that some nations may be better endowed with natural resources than others require that, whilst these inequalities can never be solved, they must at least be resolved. This could be termed the relationship between rich and poor or, to put it more comprehensively, the need to achieve "Right Human Relations"[2].

As these two rather 'large' problems suggest, whatever atmosphere of security the advanced countries enjoy is false in that they represent threats humanity can neither overcome nor run away from. That is to say, we cannot overcome the finite global natural environment by "conquering" it in a way that allows a perpetuation of current patterns of consumption. Neither can we hope to sustain a world order that confines the vast majority of humanity to dependency and relative poverty. If all were well for the societies of the wealthy advanced nations, inner social cohesion combined with unassailable economic and military power could have made self-imposed isolation from the world's poor within an oasis of prosperity feasible, if morally indefensible. This is not the case, however, for even within the advanced nations themselves, social cohesion in the form of large and wealthy middle classes is crumbling in the face of an increasingly competitive internationalised economy fuelled by job-destroying technologies.

---

[1] See *Small is Beautiful*. E.F. Schumacher. Abacus, 1974. Pages 44-51.

[2] The achievement of *Right Human Relations* is a key teaching of the "Tibetan" presented by Alice A. Bailey. These teachings are furthered through the auspices of the Lucis Trust.

The widening gaps between rich and poor, be it between the nations of North and South or within national societies, therefore form parts of the same problem: the problem of achieving Right Human Relations. That our need to confront these two world problems represents little more than plain common sense renders all the more obvious the world's current predicament as unsustainable in both human and environmental terms, as well as morally indefensible.

With the third millennium now upon us, it is as if this atmosphere of relative comfort and security, albeit false, now serves only to beckon us irresistibly and inexorably towards the recognition of these truths. That comfort and security allow us a certain space in which to both contemplate world problems and take action to solve them. We find ourselves, therefore, in a period of both contemplation and crisis. In some sense, that is perhaps as it should be. For if life has meaning, how could or should it be otherwise? If we face up to it, life represents a constant stream of problems to be confronted and resolved. If we face them properly, after a while we become more adept at confronting and resolving them, even to the point of welcoming them in the sense that every crisis is an opportunity.

The failure of current policy to bring any substantial relief to the poor in either poorer or advanced countries is leading to a widening consensus which identifies certain aspects of the capitalist system and its attendant lack of spiritual values as being the root causes of the two world problems we must now confront. As this consensus grows, so too does the wealth of ideas as to how to solve or, at least, to substantially ameliorate them. Nations should raise redistributive taxes to maintain social cohesion, or levy a tax on currency speculation, or regulate transnational corporations, or tighten environmental regulations, many of them say. Welcome though such measures may be, the trouble is that in a global free market which forces nations into competition with one another there is no way on Earth any of these solutions could possibly be implemented unilaterally. Even if implemented multi-laterally by large groups of nations, the effectiveness of such solutions remains highly questionable. For nations no longer have any substantial control over their economies, a crucial sphere of human activity that was unwittingly sacrificed at the altar of global free market ideology; an absence of control which leaves them unable even to consider implementing any policy that might incur the displeasure of internationally mobile capital.

The individual nation state has therefore become largely impotent in the face of both global capital flows and transnational corporations which, now more than ever, exploit national impotence. National impotency simply means that solutions designed for national implementation have failure already built in to them. Their implementation is possible only in the mildest and most cosmetic sense and their effect is therefore unlikely to have any significant impact on the serious environmental and social problems now faced. Indeed, solutions are effectively useless unless a way can be found to bring competing nations to co-operate with each other to ensure their undiluted implementation. For in a very real sense, the new internationalised economy has brought about a world society ruled by competition, whose sole quest is to seek out the lowest common denominator. Nations are forced to compete with one another in the battle to attract investment and maintain employment (and therefore votes); managers of businesses are forced into a mode of predatory competition in order to maintain a high price for their shares (as well as to safeguard their own jobs); previously employed public sector workers are re-employed at lower wages by newly out-sourced competing private contractors; employees compete in working longer hours to avoid falling out of favour with management; schools and pupils compete for qualifications in the hope of future employment, and so it goes on. In years past, there could have been few terms more damning than for an activity to be branded "uneconomic"[3]. Today, the identical effect is achieved if an action is deemed to be "uncompetitive" or to lead to a loss of competitiveness. Indeed, we live in an age of rugged individualism: the Age of Competition.[4]

As the insidious yet damaging effects of this age of competition permeate all levels of society, we have indeed forgotten the function and power of co-operation. Perhaps we have even forgotten what the word "co-operation" means in the sense that it is so seldom practiced that its effects have come to mean so little. But only through co-operation can nations that today compete with one another hope to solve not only our two world problems but also their own internal ones. Indeed, the competitive mind-set makes even the concept of nations, organisations or people co-operating with one another appear absurd if not positively frowned upon. But as the problems caused by excessive global competition become ever more pressing upon our own doorsteps, the need for co-operation to moderate competition becomes ever more urgent. What many seem to forget, however, is the very nature of competition itself. Not only is it a mode of behaviour in precise opposition to co-operation, it is one that makes it impossible for any participant to give it up without foregoing the potential spoils. It keeps them locked in, as if in a hypnotic trance. In the global context of an increasingly internationalised economy, all nations are participants and none can give

---

[3] See *Small is Beautiful*. E.F. Schumacher. Abacus, 1974. Page 34.

[4] The 'Age of Competition' is something that Schumacher, writing in the '70s, could only hint at: "Their [rich people's] wealth depends on making inordinately large demands on limited world resources and thus puts them on an unavoidable collision course - not primarily with the poor (who are weak and defenceless) but with other rich people." *Small is Beautiful*, Page 26.

up its competitiveness in favour of promoting social cohesion or environmental protection without sacrificing employment and access to finance. As worldwide competition intensifies still further, getting from the state of global competition amongst nations to one of global co-operation is therefore becoming an absolute priority. Indeed, it is perhaps the greatest and most necessary challenge of our age. The task, therefore, is a practical one. Quite simply, how to get from competition to co-operation: from one state to the other. This is the vital 'missing link' without which the welcome solutions now emerging from leading ecologists, counter-economists and others are likely to remain sterile and confined largely to theory. The purpose of this book is to provide that missing link. However, to provide it without some notion of the policies or solutions it might bring to fruition would make for rather sterile reading. This book therefore advances a few modest proposals of its own, not as a dogmatic blueprint, but rather to demonstrate a few of the creative possibilities the missing link provides.

This book is also intended as an "insider's guide". 'Insider' should be understood as meaning all those who have already come to recognise the capitalist system in its current form as the root of our twin problems and particularly what might be termed 'big end' capitalism in the form of markets, corporations, laws, patterns of ownership, institutions, technologies and so on that are over-sized, over-concentrated or beyond the human scale. But equally important, and inextricably linked to that system, is the widespread lack of spiritual values in society. It is for all those already sharing this view that this book is written. It is also written in the hope that, should they see the revelation of this 'missing link' to be of merit, they will respond by using it as the method through which a distillate of all their various proposed solutions or policies can come to be implemented on the largest possible scale.

PERSONAL STATEMENT

My interest in world affairs dates from about 1987 when I first read E.F. Schumacher's "Small is Beautiful", after which I found his other books to be equally enlightened and stimulating. From that point my outlook on life not so much changed, but finally started to make sense. I was, and am, fortunate enough to have been born into a family of ample financial means and a family firm in which I still work. Indeed I am what David Korten would call "a Stratos dweller"[5]. Since being bowled over by Schumacher my interest in ecology nevertheless receded against the rising tide of day to day pressures and the commitment to a young family but my new-found convictions remained intact.

Attempting since 1987 to apply what Schumacher had taught me proved interesting if rather unsuccessful. Our own family business was founded and built up principally by my late father but is owned, through his generosity, by all his five sons. I found that the model of common ownership that the Scott Bader Commonwealth represented actually expressed the philosophy my father himself sought to achieve for the family business he had created for his sons – a true working community. This aim would have been perfectly achievable had all my brothers both respected that philosophy and been willing to relinquish the monetary value of their share ownership in favour of a commonwealth company. Regrettably this proved not to be the case and culminated in one of my brothers instigating litigation against the rest of us in 1995.

---

[5] "The Cloud Minders," episode 74 of *Star Trek*, depicts a planet whose rulers devote their lives to the arts in a beautiful and peaceful city, Stratos, suspended high above the planet's desolate surface. Down below, the planet's inhabitants, the Troglytes, work in misery and violence to earn the interplanetary exchange credits used to import from other planets the luxuries the rulers enjoy on Stratos. David Korten rightly finds this imagery to be very like our present world where the rich increasingly isolate themselves from the lives of ordinary people on whose toil they depend.

Disappointment at these events led me to a kind of inner despair and to re-espouse a more materialistic and competitive mode of thinking. My mother, however, kept pressing me and urging me to higher things. This I resisted with some cynicism until finally, one day, she pressed me a step too far – an act that I can only put down to grace – causing me suddenly to experience one of those rare moments of stillness that Schumacher describes:

> "But what is wisdom? Where can it be found? Here we come to the crux of the matter: it can be read about in numerous publications but it can be found only inside oneself. To be able to find it, one has first to liberate oneself from such masters as greed and envy. The stillness following liberation – even if momentary – produces the insights of wisdom which are obtainable in no other way."[6]

It is the insight resulting from that moment of stillness which seems to me to provide a WAY of substantially solving the two world problems of which I have spoken. A way of getting from a world divided and decaying in a downward spiral of competition to one more consistent with Nature and the needs of human nature. In short, *how* to get from A to B.

It is therefore clear that a process of fundamental transformation is involved and that any such proposal for fundamental transformation must inevitably be characterised by a high degree of idealism. Some might well insist, however, that any proposal which seeks to address world problems ought surely to be one borne not of idealism but of hard-headed realism. Indeed, in this and many historic cases of conflict or difficulty, proposals for their resolution have inevitably been hotly and endlessly contested by realists and idealists, or so-called 'hawks' and 'doves':

[6] *Small is Beautiful.* E.F. Schumacher. Abacus, 1974. Pages 30-31.

"... hawks will often refer to doves as idealists, or more frequently as "empty-headed idealists" or "fuzzy-headed idealists." And they are right – not, I hope, about the empty- or fuzzy-headedness – because we are indeed idealists. For I would define the idealist as one who believes in the capacity for transformation of human nature. For whatever the other characteristics of human nature, it is precisely this capacity for transformation that is responsible for the evolution and survival of the human species. It is the hawks, the so-called realists, who are out of touch with the essence of what it means to be human, the idealistic doves whose thinking is more in accord with the reality of human nature. It is the idealists who are the realistic ones."[7]

[7] *The Different Drum.* M. Scott Peck. Arrow, 1990. Page 183.

2. Community Within and Between

The problem of achieving Right Livelihood and Right Human Relations clearly represents two fundamentally human dilemmas. After all, what could be more fundamental than how we treat the natural environment or how we fortunate ones treat those less fortunate? Both represent 'internal' and 'external' personal and human challenges in that they require a balanced moderation between our self-centred needs and those of others, be they future generations who have a right to inherit a healthy environment or those less fortunate than ourselves with whom it is our common task and happiness to achieve Right Human Relations. Both are fundamental. The environment is quite simply the prerequisite of our and our descendants' physical well-being whereas achieving Right Human Relations at all levels – local, national and global – is essential to both our physical and spiritual well-being in the sense that without it there can ultimately be neither peace nor happiness.

Reconciling our innate tendency to greed and self-centredness with a healthy environment requires our good conscience to guide us – to balance us – towards behaviour compatible with both our own needs and those of a healthy and sustainable environment. A kind of 'community' is needed between our greedy (and similarly destructive) tendencies on one side and our good conscience on the other with each moderating the other in an integrated way. In short, we need to achieve a state of community within ourselves which is likely, almost automatically, to result in a lifestyle consistent with Right Livelihood. That its achievement may not be easy should come as little surprise. Indeed, for me it remains a constant challenge I frequently fail to meet.

Similarly, in determining how we should treat one another – be we rich or poor, black or white, Jew or Muslim – or, better put, how to achieve Right Human Relations, we need to learn how to achieve community between and amongst one another. To do so, we first need to understand the meaning of the word "community" because it seems to have lost or changed its meaning over time. Indeed, so much abused has it become, it risks getting a bad name for itself.[1] The type of community referred to here is quite different. Perhaps it can best be defined firstly by describing its antithesis: the "rugged individualism" that has become the hallmark of the Age of Competition:

> "…the ideal of rugged individualism encourages us to fake it. It encourages us to hide our weaknesses and failures. It teaches us to be utterly ashamed of our limitations. It drives us to attempt to be superwomen and supermen not only in the eyes of others but also in our own. It pushes us day in and day out to look as if we 'had it all together', as if we were without needs and in total control of our lives. It also relentlessly isolates us from each other. And it makes genuine community impossible. …
>
> In our culture of rugged individualism – in which we generally feel that we dare not be honest about ourselves…– we bandy around the word 'community'. We apply it to almost any collection of individuals – a town, a church, a synagogue, a fraternal organization, an apartment complex, a professional association – regardless of how poorly those individuals communicate with each other. It is a false use of the word.

[1] I am referring here to the UK Conservative policy called "Care in the Community" in which inmates, some dangerous, were released from secure hospitals in the vain hope that they would be adequately cared for 'in the community', occasionally with tragic results.

If we are going to use the word meaningfully we must restrict it to a group of individuals who have learned how to communicate honestly with each other, whose relationships go deeper than their masks of composure, and who have developed some significant commitment to 'rejoice together, mourn together,' and to 'delight in each other, make others' conditions our own.' "[2]

To achieve such a state of community with others in this deep sense, we need first to recognise our own prejudices and hobby horses and see them for what they usually are: pure ego. If we can do so and detach ourselves from them, we come to see that what we so easily recognise in others as egotistical prejudices are little different from our own. They become, as it were, part of us. For as we recognise ourselves in others, we can start to love others as we love ourselves, however different from us they may appear. In fact we come to love and celebrate their, as well as our, 'differentness'. In the context of international relations, on the other hand, whilst politicians freely talk of the "international community", nations cannot be said to demonstrate any particular desire to form themselves into anything remotely resembling a true community of nations. In fact, the reverse is nearer the truth. This is no more obvious than the way in which advanced nations dominate and exclude non-industrialised and poor nations:

"...the bulk of the world's population live in closed worlds, trapped by the lottery of their birth. For the average worker or farmer with a family, one's nation state is a community of fate. ... Internationally open cultures and rooted populations present an explosive contradiction... As the advanced countries seek to police the movement of the world's poor and exclude them, the capriciousness of the notions of citizenship and of political community will become ever more evident. Advanced states will not be able effectively to use as

[2] *The Different Drum*. M. Scott Peck. Arrow, 1990.

a principle of exclusion the claim to cultural homogeneity – for they are ethnically and culturally pluralistic. Exclusion will be a mere fact, with no other logic or legitimacy than that states are fearful of the consequences of large-scale migration. A world of wealth and poverty, with appalling and widening differences in living standards between the richest and the poorest nations, is unlikely to be secure or stable." [3]

Indeed, the need for community amongst nations - the need to cease competition and commence co-operation - grows ever more urgent. And here we come to the point: that the stages individuals must travel to get from the state of rugged individualism to that of community are remarkably similar to those that nations too must travel if they are to move from competition to co-operation. These four stages, as identified and explained by Scott Peck, merit describing here because they are profoundly relevant to the dynamics of what is proposed in this book.

THE FOUR STAGES OF COMMUNITY

When individuals previously unknown to one another voluntarily come together in Scott Peck's "community-building work-shops" to achieve that deeper sense of community, there are four distinct and consecutive stages that usually occur. These work-shops take place over the course of two or three days, by the end of which it is hoped that the final stage of 'community' will have been achieved:

Pseudocommunity can be described merely as the reaction of a group of people who are seeking to form a community and start off, as soon as they meet, by pretending they already are one. They try to fake it by attempting to be an instant community in being extremely pleasant and polite with one another and going to great lengths to avoid any disagreements.

[3] *Globalization in Question.* Paul Hirst & Grahame Thompson. Polity Press, 1996.

Chaos is the period when the cloying politeness and pleasantness of pseudocommunity finally gives way to the participants revealing their true prejudices and irritations about each other. This manifests itself as well-intentioned but misguided and competitive attempts to heal and convert:

> "After a period of uneasy silence a member will say, 'Well, the reason I came to this workshop is that I have such-and-such a problem, and I thought I might find a solution to it here.'
> 'I had that problem once,' a second member will respond. 'I did such-and-such, and it took care of the difficulty.'
> 'Well, I tried that,' the first member answers, 'but it didn't solve anything.'
> 'When I acknowledged Jesus to be my Lord and Savior,' a third member announces, 'it took care of that problem and every other problem I had.'
> 'I'm sorry,' says the first member, 'but that Jesus Lord-and-Savior stuff just doesn't grab me. It's not where I'm at.'
> 'No,' says a fourth member. 'As a matter of fact, it makes me want to puke.'
> 'But it's true,' proclaims a fifth member.
> And so they're off.
> By and large, people resist change. So the healers and converters try harder to heal or convert, until finally their victims get their backs up and start trying to heal the healers and convert the converters. It is indeed chaos.
>
> Chaos is not just a state, it is an essential part of the process of community development. Consequently, unlike pseudocommunity, it does not simply go away as soon as the group becomes aware of it. In the stage of chaos individual differences are, unlike those in pseudocommunity, right out in the open. Only now, instead of trying to hide or ignore them, the group is attempting to obliterate them. Underlying the attempts to heal and convert is not so much the motive of love as the motive to make everyone *normal*-and the motive to win, as the members fight over whose norm might prevail."[4]

Emptiness is the stage at which the participants come gradually to realise the futility of their chaotic and competitive attempts at healing and converting one another. In Scott Peck's community-building process, he will often invite his group to enter the stage of emptiness:

> "More often than not the group will simply ignore me and go on squabbling. Then after another while I will say, 'I suggested to you that the only way from chaos to community is into and through emptiness. But apparently you were not terribly interested in my suggestion.' More squabbling, but finally a member will ask with a note of annoyance, 'Well, what is this emptiness stuff anyway?'
>
> It is no accident that groups are not generally eager to pick up on my suggestion of emptiness. The fact that 'emptiness' is a mystical sort of word and concept is not the deterrent. People are smart, and often in the dimmer recesses of their consciousness they know more than they want to know. As soon as I mention 'emptiness,' they have a presentiment of what is to come. And they are in no hurry to accept it.
>
> Emptiness is the hard part. It is also the bridge between chaos and community."[5]

In entering emptiness the members of the group come to recognise both the futility of their attempts at healing and converting and the hypocrisy of their self-righteousness as being no better nor more nobly motivated than those of others. In so doing, they eventually exhaust their attempts, emptying themselves of barriers such as expectations, preconceptions, prejudices, ideologies and their need to control others: the barriers to communication that prevent the onset of community.

With the death that emptiness gradually brings to these barriers, the state of *Community* itself is attained:

[4] *The Different Drum.* M. Scott Peck. Arrow, 1990. Pages 90-91.
[5] *The Different Drum.* M. Scott Peck. Arrow, 1990. Pages 94-95.

"In this final stage a soft quietness descends. It is a kind of peace. The room is bathed in peace. Then, quietly, a member [of the group] begins to talk about herself. She is being very vulnerable. She is speaking of the deepest part of herself. The group hangs on each word. No one realized she was capable of such eloquence.

When she is finished there is a hush. It goes on a long time. But it does not seem long. There is no uneasiness in this silence. Slowly, out of the silence, another member begins to talk. He too is speaking very deeply, very personally, about himself. He is not trying to heal or convert the first person. He's not even trying to respond to her. It's not she but he who is the subject. Yet the other members of the group do not sense he has ignored her...

A third member speaks. Perhaps it will be to respond to the previous speaker, but there will be in this response no attempt to heal or convert. It may be a joke, but it will not be at anyone's expense. It may be a short poem that is almost magically appropriate. It could be anything soft and gentle, but again it will be a gift.

Then the next member speaks. And as it goes on, there will be a great deal of sadness and grief expressed; but there will also be much laughter and joy. There will be tears in abundance. Sometimes, simultaneously, they will be tears of both. And then something almost more singular happens. An extraordinary amount of healing and converting begins to occur – now that no one is trying to convert or heal. And community has been born."[6]

These stages are of profound importance for they represent a very human truth: the truth of reconciliation. Just as they apply to a group of people voluntarily coming together to bring themselves to emptiness in order to achieve Community, so similar stages apply to the process of moving from competition to co-operation. They are analogous

6 *The Different Drum*. M. Scott Peck. Arrow, 1990. Page 103.

whether it concerns either a group of individuals that compete with one another over a particular point of view or a world of nations competing with one another in the global economy. As economic aspects of human relations become ever more globalised, so the recognition of the Earth's natural limits and humanity's consequent need and capacity for trans-formation - from chaos to community or from competition to co-operation – seems destined to become the central theme in the unavoidable confrontation with his two world problems. For when life becomes global, we start not only to see the impossibility of escape from that confrontation but the very real need for humanity to engage it whole-hearted-ly and with determination.

Like each human being, the nations of the world too could be said to be at a certain stage in their community development. With global communications and media broad-casting it is indeed now possible to talk of a world society or world consciousness. As television or the Internet serve to bring the reality of inequalities right into our front rooms, the self-awareness of world society will continue to become stronger and more in focus.

> "The impoverished can watch 'Dallas'. They know another world is possible, whether they are watching it in a slum apart-ment in an advanced country or a shanty town in a Third World country. The ideology of socialist revolution may have few takers but one should not imagine that the world's poor will remain cowed or passively accept their poverty. The responses, whether of street crime or guerilla struggles like Chiapas, will be far harder to cope with than old-style com-munist-directed revolts."[7]

Be it the poor that know what could be possible, or the rich that fear what the poor aspire to, both give strength to the necessity of achieving a true World Community. In the

[7] *Globalization in Question.* Hirst & Thompson. Polity Press, 1996.

community building process, however, since jumping or skipping any of its stages is impossible, it is perhaps worth considering at what stage in that process the world now finds itself today. Indeed, it is arguable that a distinct and quite identifiable evolutionary process of world community development could be said to exist and to be unfolding. The illumination of this wider perspective on world events and history is important in considering the action that might now be appropriate in addressing the two world problems confronting us.

3. Undercurrents of Global Community Development

Insofar as global free markets reign supreme the world remains in chaos. However, it should be remembered that it was our political leaders who deliberately de-regulated markets in the first place. That they did so is therefore somewhat irrelevant to 'where the world is at' in terms of its community development or its collective conscience. For even though the increasingly competitive international economy exacerbates our two world problems, that is something quite different from what people think or feel. It is, I believe, true to speak of a strong under-current of world consciousness and community development, both of which become more visible if we tap into the under-currents of world history.

One could briefly trace the stages of development of world community as they relate to the community-building process as follows:

PSEUDOCOMMUNITY

This could encompass the period prior to the formation of nation states. No doubt it was also a period of much chaos. However in world terms that chaos was insignificant in that wars or man's impact on his environment or his level of economic development were largely locally confined and therefore limited and fragmented in impact.

As nation states gradually formed into the patchwork we are more familiar with, we can see how this patchwork had dramatic effects both between states and upon the populations within them:

"In the seventeenth century the modern states system was created and mutually recognised by its members. Central to that recognition was that each state was the sole political authority with exclusive possession of a defined territory. The 'state' became the dominant form of government, accepting no other agency as rival. The Middle Ages had known no such singular relationship between authority and territory. ...

The modern state did not acquire its monopoly of governance by its own internal efforts alone. After the Treaty of Westphalia in 1648 governments ceased to support co-religionists in conflict with their own states. The mutual recognition by states of each other's sovereignty in the most important contemporary matter, religious belief, meant that states were willing to forgo certain political objectives in return for internal control and stability. ...Thus to a significant degree the capacity for sovereignty came from without, through agreements between states in the newly emerging society of states."[1]

Expressed in terms of a community-building process, we could thus identify the entity of the nation state as representing the equivalent of the individual person: the prime agent through which community or chaos in the world will ultimately be determined.

CHAOS

Since the birth of the society of states in the seventeenth century, their development has been a gradual evolution of individual national identities. Having secured internal control over their respective populations, nation states then sought first to develop and then to externalise that identity by attempting to exert control and domination over other states mainly through war. Thus the era (or stage) of chaos commenced and evolved through regular wars between

---

[1] *Globalization in Question.* Paul Hirst & Grahame Thompson. Polity Press, 1996. Page 171.

European states as well as during the subsequent colonisation process in other continents.

This era of chaos could be said to equate to what M. Scott Peck identifies as the competitive urge to heal and convert in the community-building process. Whilst the notion of healing and converting may have been far from the minds of those waging war or plundering colonies, the underlying spiritual motivation was nevertheless the same: a desire, belief or prejudice in favour of the supremacy of the aggressor's particular national (i.e. self) identity. For many decades such wars were embarked upon regularly and seemingly without a moment's hesitation. However, as time passed, diplomacy played an increasingly important role reflecting a gradual move towards the possibility of negotiation as an alternative and preferable means of resolving conflict. As war gave way to diplomacy, so war and colonisation gave way to economic exploitation as a less overtly violent means of domination.

To the extent that the current world order is today primarily dictated by the triad of northern nations consisting of the USA, EU and Japan amongst whom the risk of war has receded to the point of insignificance, it could perhaps be said that the era of world chaos was drawing to a close with the end of the Cold War in 1989. The necessity of its closing became all the more obvious by the futility (and loss) of the Vietnam War by the world's strongest military power: the United States. By way of further confirmation, it is perhaps no coincidence that conflicts such as Apartheid in South Africa which, had it occurred in an earlier era, would most likely have resulted in mass loss of life, were in the end settled largely peacefully. Naturally, this does not mean that war is over – regrettably far from it. But somehow, from a northern triad perspective, violent conflict that does occur, be it the invasion of Kuwait by Iraq or the ethnic cleansing of the Balkans, seems today to be completely out of step or anachronistic to us. Even the most deeply endemic historical conflicts such as Northern Ireland or the Middle East seem to be slowly succumbing to the realisation that the era of violent chaos is drawing to a close and that the era of emptiness beckons. An important early symbol calling for the closure of the period of chaos was perhaps the founding of the United Nations at the end of World War II.

I believe it is generally true to say, therefore, that the evolving undercurrent of world community development is at a spiritual watershed hovering uncertainly between chaos and emptiness. The concept of mass loss of life and destruction has become largely unthinkable and unacceptable to the northern dominated world order and the great ideological struggles to achieve broad acceptance in principle (if not in practice) of racial, sexual and religious respect and tolerance as well as the paramount importance of peace, democracy and human rights are, from a western perspective, now over.

EMPTINESS OR MORE CHAOS?

What might have been an opportunity to move more decisively into the era of emptiness was perhaps missed in the 1970s. The decade, at least from a western perspective, represented something of a cultural and spiritual vacuum having nothing of the energy, style and raw idealism of the 1960s and it failed to offer anything of substance in replacement. This colluded with the arms race and the Cold War to freeze the further evolution of world community development. Public awareness of environmental issues had not yet taken root despite dramatic post-war economic growth, rapidly increasing resource use and growing evidence of pollution. Similarly, the preoccupation of northern advanced countries with the more immediate threat posed by the arms race served to distract public attention from the suffering of poorer southern nations. As the burgeoning economic expansion of the 1960s gave way to recessions in the 1970s, a vacuum in economic ideology also developed leaving some economists – the emerging gurus of the post-war elite – only too ready to offer prescriptions.

It was against this backdrop of '70s cultural doldrum and economic vacuum that the ideology of global free markets found fertile ground in which to germinate and take root.[2] Instead of listening to the voices of those such as Fritz Schumacher, (articulated in "Small is Beautiful" which remains as valid today as it was when published in 1974), neo-liberal economists had by the early 1980s offered world leaders an entirely more glamorous and grander vision.

THE GOLDEN MERRY-GO-ROUND

And so it was, once upon a time, that the children who should lead the world were brought to a beautiful fairground. In it stood just one single yet enormous ride, the size and beauty of which they had never witnessed before: the golden merry-go-round. The outside was painted in the most wondrous colours and decorated in multi-coloured fairy lights. Strings of gold coins hung from the ceiling and they tinkled and jangled around the heads of the horses. The inner core was made of pure gold and incorporated a grand accordion from which emanated the intoxicating chimes telling of a glorious ride to global prosperity.

Being an insider's guide, the reader is spared repetition of the detailed consequences wrought on nations of all types by global free markets. The analogy of a merry-go-round is appropriate because, as it spins ever faster, it exemplifies the centrifugal force that weighs heavier the further from the

---

[2] The importance of corporate funded right-wing 'think tanks' in formulating and disseminating free-market policies to right-of-centre political parties is well documented in chapter 5 of *Global Spin - The Corporate Assault on Environmentalism*. Sharon Beder. Green Books, 1997.

core one sits. The advanced countries, of course, sit nearest the core shielded from the worst effects whilst benefiting from the more harmful effects on others. Developing countries, on the other hand, sit on the outer horses, struggling to hang on. The countries are locked in competition with one another to sit on the horses nearest the centre. Countries that have suffered in one way or another spring instantly to mind: Britain, Sweden, New Zealand, Mexico, the south east Asian 'Tigers', Brazil. Where next? And this is to say nothing of the non-industrialised countries who, starved of capital, are left to the real misery and chaos of warfare, famine, poverty and spiraling numbers of refugees.

Whilst the world becomes ever more spiritually ready to take the crucial step into an era of emptiness in which the exclusion of less industrialised and non-industrialised countries as well as problems within advanced countries might be addressed, it instead finds itself caught in the grip of a new form of economic chaos, the full consequences of which are yet to be fully realised. Realisation is particularly lacking in those advanced countries situated at the core of the merry-go-round where its centrifugal force is less powerful. Developing nations on the periphery, however, such as Mexico or Brazil, are coming to realise the consequences of chaos more clearly.[3] Addicted as they are to the drip feed of dependency-inducing foreign debt administered by the "West knows best" doctors at the World Bank and the IMF, it remains unclear whether they can ever free themselves from the vicious threat of the wrecking ball.[4]

A growing chorus of calls amongst some economic experts for re-regulation of free markets can now be heard for

[3] See *Mexico's Coming Backlash*, M. Delal Baer in Foreign Affairs, July/August 1999.
[4] In *The Crisis of Global Capitalism*, (Little, Brown & Co. 1998) Geoge Soros likens the flight of capital during a crisis to a wrecking ball swinging wildly from the crane of a demolition vehicle.

what would be an attempt to 'cool the casino'[5]. Whether such calls can ultimately overwhelm the neo-liberalist free market fundamentalists remains to be seen. If they succeed, increased control of the international economy will provide some measure of relief. However, it will do little to ameliorate the dire human and social consequences of mass unemployment wrought by ever more rapid technological change driven by computerisation particularly in robotics and in many service sector functions. This all the more so under the tutelage of a debt-based financial system that ensures that only the rich get richer. These dire effects are, however, not confined to the poor nations of the South. Incontrovertible evidence of unravelling social cohesion within advanced northern societies is already becoming hard for policy makers to ignore.

GLOBAL MARKET "DICTATORSHIP"

There are two central but inter-linked problems this book seeks to address. Firstly, that unregulated global capital markets represent a supra-national power that subtly but effectively regulates the policies of national governments: a situation that has engendered political and economic paralysis from which we cannot ordinarily escape. A global regulatory framework for capital markets is therefore essential. Secondly, that the social and environmental consequences of leaving transnational corporations (TNCs) to exploit national governments against the back-drop of that paralysis can only accelerate both the growing division between rich and poor as well as the continued degradation of the environment. Whilst a regulatory framework is doubtless essential, the main factor working against it is competition: competition between nation states and competition between TNCs. In analysing these problems, we can see how the

[5] *Globalization in Question*. Hirst & Thompson. Polity Press, 1996. Page 135.

forces of competition are coming to represent the core barrier to creating that framework.

Taking the first of these problems, the unpredictability and volatility of world markets itself acts as a severe constraint upon the freedom of action of the nation state:

> "...governments often cannot know whether the response of world markets to their policies will be merely to make them costly or to render them completely unworkable. Governments are in a situation in which even the span of options that is available to them is uncertain. This continuing radical uncertainty is the most disabling constraint on the power of sovereign states."[6]

> "The policy options open to nation-states in the 1990s are not delivered to them as a menu with fixed prices. The governments of sovereign states do not know in advance how markets will react. There are few, if any, rules of monetary or fiscal rectitude whose violation will result in predictable penalties. At the margin, no doubt, policies that are ultra-risky in terms of inflation or government debt, say, will be punished by watchful bond markets; but the scale of severity of such market responses cannot be known in advance. National governments in the 1990s are flying blind."[7]

The inherent uncertainty of international de-regulated capital markets tends to engineer a kind of paralysis of national economic policy ensuring governments' adherence only to policies they can be sure will not displease world markets. These are necessarily free-market policies characterised by weak environmental and labour regulations: policies which serve only to intensify the very serious social, economic and environmental problems the world now faces. For politicians to risk venturing beyond the narrow policy parameters acceptable to capital markets would likely result in

6 *False Dawn*. John Gray. Granta Books, 1999.
7 *False Dawn*. John Gray. Granta Books, 1999.

capital flight with its attendant consequences of devaluation, inflation and unemployment: a venture only the politically suicidal could contemplate. For today, the pursuit of national economic success is no longer an absolute but a *relative* undertaking. The effectiveness of a government's policies upon its nation is now largely determined by economic, social, taxation and other conditions prevailing in *other* neighbouring or competing nations. The constraints imposed by the ability of capital to cross borders at will, combined with the ability of corporations to move production and therefore employment to lower cost countries, thus abandons nation states to a competitive struggle to attract capital and maintain employment – and therefore votes. In the absence of any significant international control over world markets, the economic role of government is thus confined to the relentless pursuit only of those policies which both garner market approval and favour business in an effort to maintain national competitiveness against other nations:

> "In this new rivalry American free markets work to undercut both European and Asian social market economics. This is despite the fact that the social costs of business are borne in different ways in European and Asian social markets. Both are threatened by the American model because each business bears social obligations that in the United States it has shed. At the same time Chinese capitalism is emerging as a rival to the American version because it can go further than the American free market in undercutting social markets in Europe and the rest of Asia.
>
> All the familiar models of market institutions are mutating as global competition is played out through the structures of sovereign states. It is a basic error to think that this is a contest that any of the existing models can win."[8]

[8] *False Dawn.* John Gray. Granta Books, 1999. Feeling they are no longer competitive, continental European states are compelled to downgrade regulation to bring themselves down to (or below) the level of their economic rivals. See *The Independent*, 24th June 1999: "GERMANY is starting to cut back the size of the state."

"A global free market works to set sovereign states against one another in geo-political struggles for dwindling natural resources. The effect of a *laissez-faire* philosophy which condemns state intervention in the economy is to impel states to become rivals for control of resources that no institution has any responsibility for conserving. Nor, evidently, does a world economy that is organized as a global free market meet the universal human need for security. A regime of global *laissez-faire* that prevents governments from discharging this protective role is creating the conditions for still greater political, and economic, instability."[9]

Unlike previous experiments when free markets were of a scale that allowed their re-regulation, the present scale, reach and mobility of international trade and capital markets puts them beyond national re-regulation. For if any nation or group of nations were to attempt it, capital would flee those countries causing currency devaluation and higher inflation, if not outright economic collapse. Furthermore, in moving elsewhere, the markets would only carry on as before. Global capital markets are therefore beyond the control of individual or even groups of nations. To the extent that politicians today are able neither to flout the narrow policy parameters global markets dictate nor to re-regulate them, they are effectively subject to a supra-national power or, one might even say, to a quasi-dictatorship. This is the critical point we must now recognise. The policies subtly but effectively imposed by global free markets and international competition thus become irreversible as John Gray points out, taking New Zealand as an example:

"Most decisively, the restructuring of New Zealand's economy which opened it to unregulated capital flows conferred on transnational capital an effective veto power over public policy. Wherever public policies might be perceived as impacting

[9] *False Dawn*. John Gray. Grant Books, 1999.

upon competitiveness, profits and economic stability they could be quashed by the threat of capital flight. Neo-liberal reforms thereby became politically irreversible."[10]

Hans-Peter Martin and Harald Schumann also graphically describe the difficulties the nation state faces in exerting any kind of influence or control. In this instance they refer to the "Tobin Tax" which proposes a 1% tax on all currency dealing transactions in order to throw a little 'sand in the wheels' of global currency speculation:

"Theoretically and politically, there has for years been no argument against Tobin's proposal that is worth taking seriously. Indeed, it 'cannot be faulted theoretically,' in the view of Hans-Helmut Kotz, chief economist at Germany's Girozentrale, the central national savings institution. But the simple scheme obviously has one drawback: those who would be affected by it are resolutely opposed and, as in the case of ordinary taxes, they play off the nations of the world against one another. Kotz: 'New York and London will always block it.' But if just one major financial centre were free of the tax, the currency trade would gravitate there. And even if the G-7 countries all introduced a Tobin tax, the financial sector could formally switch its business to offshore branches from the Cayman Islands to Singapore and so undermine the intended restricting effect. Failure is therefore 'programmed into' such a tax on currency transactions, an economist at the Deutsche Bank cheerfully predicts. One of his American colleagues dotted the 'i's' on the threat. If the state starts interfering in the trade, 'we'll eventually be financial organizations headquartered on a ship floating mid-ocean' ".[11]

In the face of such threats, our political leaders throw their hands up in helplessness and inaction:

[10] *False Dawn.* John Gray. Grant Books, 1999.
[11] *The Global Trap.* Martin & Schumann. Zed Books, 1997. Pages 83-84.

"Tobin's proposal is 'no longer applicable today,' State Secretary Jurgen Stark says to justify the fiscal inaction against speculators. It would work only 'if it was [introduced] by all 190 countries in the world.'"[12]

Some argue that nation states still have options to control capital flows and thus to protect their economies citing Malaysia or Chile as examples. But I suggest that these exceptions merely serve to prove the rule. After all, those countries only imposed capital controls when faced with the direct threat of imminent economic crisis such as the South American or South-East Asian crises and therefore had little to lose by taking that action. Those circumstances can hardly be compared to the economies of the major industrialised countries who face, and are unlikely ever to face, any such threat. Indeed, it is highly questionable whether even the G-7 countries acting together could risk contemplating such action for fear of capital fleeing to Hong Kong, Zurich or other non-G-7 financial centres. It is therefore necessary, I believe, to face the reality that, by and large, capital controls can be imposed only in the exceptional case when the consequences of imminent economic crisis effectively mean the country concerned has less to lose by imposing such controls than by not doing so: i.e. when it is clearly the lesser of two evils. Barring a financial crisis of truly global proportions, such a situation is unlikely ever to arise for the G-7.

PSEUDO-DEMOCRACY SUPPLANTS DEMOCRACY

As international competition gradually intensifies, the overall effect is becoming increasingly clear: that the constraints on policy imposed by de-regulated global financial markets and TNCs combined with governments' inability to re-regulate

[12] *The Global Trap.* Martin & Schumann. Zed Books, 1997.

them mean that our political leaders have unwittingly yet irrevocably sacrificed not only their power to influence the economy but the very quality of democracy itself. Since the pursuit of national economic success is now a relative undertaking, policies involving higher taxation and public spending or measures that seek to protect the environment thus increasing the costs of industry have consequently become substantially unworkable:

> "...the ups and downs of freely convertible currencies reflect the expectations of future growth and competitiveness that investors entertain about the respective economies. In a way, a country's whole economy thus becomes a commodity, whose relative value crystallizes through the return envisaged by investment fund managers. This gives the finance markets great power vis-à-vis economically weak countries, so great that the fluctuations in the exchange rate can decide the fate of whole nations. Governments, whether democratic or authoritarian, often find themselves compelled to gear their economic, social and fiscal policies to the interests of investors, with the result that the interest of their own people in social and economic security all too easily goes by the board."[13]

> "The effect of competition from countries in which a regime of deregulation, low taxes and a shrinking welfare state has been imposed is to force downwards harmonization of policies on states which retain social market economies. ... The workings of the global bond markets reduce or remove from the world's social markets much of the freedom their governments had in the past to pursue counter-cyclical policies. They force them to return to a pre-Keynsian situation in which they have few effective levers of macroeconomic management. ... Global capital markets...make social democracy unviable."[14]

[13] *Planet Dialectics.* Wolfgang Sachs. Zed Books, 1999.
[14] *False Dawn.* John Gray. Granta Books, 1998.

By their inability to deviate from these policy constraints, governments of whatever party and their electorates must now submit to what are, effectively, permanent political conditions. Conditions in which whatever party we elect, the policies we receive inevitably conform to market and corporate demands and not necessarily to what the electorate desires. Little wonder, therefore, that "recent experiences in many countries show that there are no substantial differences in the policies towards finance capital whether the governments in power are left or right."[15]

Certainly electorates around the world still generally believe they live in truly democratic countries, a misapprehension which is leading to a marked and increasing mis-match between voter expectations and political-economic reality. Voters are led to believe that in selecting a particular party they are voting for a particular political approach. But they become confused when, once in power, their party fails to deliver what they might have expected. This mis-match is proving problematic particularly for political parties on the centre-left. Once they gain power, their traditional supporters, particularly trade unions, are left scratching their heads, failing to understand why their party, now in power, seems curiously reluctant to implement its traditional policies or to listen seriously to their needs:

> "The macroeconomic climate has been as inhospitable to unions as the microeconomy of individual firms. Widespread government deregulation in the 1980s, combined with high levels of government debt in the 1990s, increased governments' reliance on international financial markets and gave those markets increased leverage over the economic policies adopted by individual nations. But global financial markets tend to shy away from precisely the kinds of policies that unions have traditionally advocated - full employment, high growth, and a

---

[15] *A Citizen's Guide to the Globalization of Finance.* Kavaljit Singh. Zed Books, 1999.

tendency to lower interest rates and increased public spending when employment rates flag. The threat of capital flight (and the ensuing currency devaluations and higher inflation) and the desire to attract international capital to finance deficits and spur economic growth have prompted even center-left governments to turn a deaf ear to union preferences."[16]

This explains why, at a time when the gap between rich and poor is perhaps at its greatest, when job security is at its weakest and when the political left around the world should consequently be at the peak of its effectiveness, it instead finds itself effectively neutered by the political effects of global free markets and international competition. Far from being at its peak, therefore, the traditional left is instead struggling to find a role for itself in a political-economic environment in which its traditional policies have become impracticable. For any political party, impractical policies inevitably spell political redundancy and a loss of support. In the struggle against redundancy, therefore, the left has had little option but to shed those traditional policies; the policies that once defined its socialist identity – its very ethos. In doing so, the democratic political choice they represented to the electorate has consequently been permanently excluded from the political scene. By shedding those policies, traditional centre-left parties such as Old Labour or its counterparts in other countries have been forced to re-position themselves (under the cover of 'Third Way' or other appropriate spin) more towards the right: just where the market determines that they, or any other party seeking power, must be. In doing so, they have inevitably adopted most of the economic policies traditionally pursued by centre-right parties. Whilst centre-left parties have sold their souls by moving to the right, traditional

---

[16] *Workers of the World, Now What?* By Kathleen Newland, senior associate at the Carnegie Endowment for International Peace and codirector of its International Migration Policy Program. Quoted from *Foreign Policy*, Spring 1999.

centre-right parties equally have a problem: the problem of finding themselves displaced and politically redundant as a consequence of the neo-liberal policies their predecessors previously implemented. As former UK Prime Minister John Major once put it:

> "I went swimming leaving my clothes on the bank and when I came back Tony Blair was wearing them."[17]

Indeed, we should perhaps ask ourselves what is the purpose and function of centre-right parties when so-called centre-left parties across Europe and elsewhere – according to market/corporate demands - are successfully delivering traditional centre-right economic policies in any case?

It is as if democracy could be portrayed as a theatre stage with politicians and their parties as the actors spread across the stage from left to right. In proper democratic conditions, the spotlights would light the entire stage giving the audience (i.e. the electorate) a clear and illuminated view or choice across the entire political spectrum. The fierce competition between nation states engendered by globally mobile capital and corporations has however interfered with the lighting system such that only the right half of the stage remains illuminated leaving the left in total darkness and its actors invisible. Both the actors finding themselves shrouded in darkness and the electorate seeing a restricted stage thus unwittingly and automatically shift their stance or gaze towards the illuminated area of the stage on the right. Whilst the shift of traditional left-of-centre parties towards the right is usually seen merely as a function of party-political expediency, we should

---

[17] *The Week*, Issue 227, 23rd October 1999. It should also be noted that the policy convergence described often leaves taxation as the only area of policy available for party-political differentiation. This results in tax-cutting competitions in the run-ups to elections which serve only to further weaken public services and wealth redistribution. See *The Guardian*, 15th March 2000: "Low tax a moral duty, says Hague....Hague outlined his aim of making tax a key election battleground,...".

therefore be aware of the underlying anti-democratic forces at work. As such, those voters to the left of centre are today effectively deprived of political expression and of their democratic rights.

Many advocates of free markets point to the spread or *quantity* of democracy that market deregulation has encouraged around the world. This may be so. However, at the same time, the narrowing of the freedom of action of the nation state that free markets dictate serves to degrade the *quality* of democracy. The will of the people has thus become subordinate to the will of the markets. Democracy has in fact been reduced to a kind of pseudo-democracy: one in which the people are duped into thinking they have a political choice when, in fact, they don't. The traditional view of democracy led us to believe that different political parties would each deliver different policies once elected. Under pseudo-democracy, however, what we inevitably receive are the same free-market, neo-liberal, business-friendly policies merely 'spun' in different clothing.

Indeed, we must now accept that in the era of globalisation, conventional party politics, *regardless* of the party in government, is substantially unable to deviate from the neo-liberal policies demanded by global markets, TNCs and competition and the sooner we all wake up to the fact of this political paralysis and its serious implications the better.

The rapid spread around the world of "democracy" is perhaps no accident. As the TNCs spread their activities globally into the developing world, they need political and social stability to carry on their businesses. With global financial markets ensuring the establishment of pseudo-democracy in all so-called democratic countries, the new economic elite consisting of TNCs and shareholders along with the IMF, World Bank and WTO who support their agenda, no longer needs to prop up unpopular dictators in order to secure a stable penetration of developing markets. With electorates around the world suitably brainwashed by pseudo-democracy into thinking they have a real choice, the policies the elite requires are delivered without the social, political unrest and instability normally associated with dictators and military juntas. To look, therefore, to party politics for solutions to domestic problems (let alone world ones) has become substantially futile.

Let us now turn to the second but related problem of the growing power that TNCs are able to wield against a backdrop of market-induced government impotence. There can be little doubt that major corporations, and in particular transnational corporations, constitute the main force in the global economy for goods and services and are consequently responsible for much of the physical effects that economic activity has on the environment.

> "The corporations control 'between a quarter and a third of all world production and are particularly active in processing and marketing', according to the Brandt Report in 1980: 'The marketing, processing or production of several commodities – including bauxite, copper, iron ore, nickel, lead, zinc, tin, tobacco, bananas and tea – is dominated in each case by a small number of transnational corporations.' The extent of their activities has since become much higher. It is common for a small number of TNCs to account for over 80 per cent of the trade in agricultural products.... .'Outside the primary sector, upwards of two thirds of the world's exports of goods and services are accounted for by TNCs; and 30-40 per cent of these take place within the same institutions.' One estimate suggests that the biggest 500 TNCs 'control about 70 per cent of world trade, 80 per cent of foreign investment and about 30 per cent of world GDP'."[18]

Against a background of world markets beyond national control, corporations operating internationally are ideally

---

[18] *Big Business - Poor Peoples.* John Madeley. Zed Books, 1999.

placed to take advantage of any country playing off one against another by exploiting the preoccupation of every nation with maintaining employment:

> "Senior Ford executives yesterday urged the Prime Minister to commit more state aid to a key British plant to prevent 1,400 jobs being lost. At a 30-minute meeting in Downing Street, the company told Tony Blair that the £30m in government subsidy…did not match the sums available elsewhere. It is understood that the German and Spanish governments have indicated that more generous packages might be available for plants in Cologne and Valencia. …
>
> Ken Jackson, the general secretary of the Amalgamated Engineering and Electrical Union, expressed confidence that the Government and the company would arrive at a deal: 'Bridgend is a productive plant with an excellent, highly skilled workforce. I'm sure the investment needed to produce the new engine will be secured,' he said. …
>
> A Ford spokesman said yesterday's talks … were the kind which took place in every country Ford was involved in."[19]

In exploiting national governments in this way, TNCs can both obtain free government subsidies at tax payers' expense and can, either directly or through the auspices of the World Trade Organisation, deter or prevent governments from imposing stricter employment conditions or environmental regulations thus securing ever-higher profits for their share-holders. They can also draw trade unions in to playing their game which unions willingly do, if somewhat uneasily, in order to safeguard their members' interests. This adds a false but compelling air of legitimacy to the case put by the cor-porations. With governments fearing a loss of votes, unions fearing a loss of membership and employees fearing for their continued employment it all amounts to a neat trick that governments of whatever party can ill afford to question for

---

[19] *The Independent.* 29th May 1999.

fear of the corporation concerned moving production else-where. Their willingness to acquiesce in this game is under-standable, for with other nations only too ready to welcome any corporation ready to set up a new factory, not to play would be self-defeating and would lay governments open to the charge of not acting in the "national interest".

POLITICAL LEADERS

And so we see how our political leaders who are commonly regarded as being in a position of power (and who doubtless believe themselves to be in control), are in fact very much guided by, and subject to, global pressures far beyond their control. Indeed there are severe difficulties for our leaders, for it is impossible for them to go out on a limb and recognise the needs of the future any distance beyond what the accepted view of the possibilities are amongst the people for whose support they are competing. Politics, like everything else, has become a sort of game with an accepted agenda, a mainstream agenda, and any attempt to step outside it will result in marginalisation. Our leaders cannot risk advocating policies or views which dilute the perception of the national interest in any way. If they did so, their opponents or the people with the daggers standing behind them are ready to get rid of them and take their place. As such our leaders are prisoners within a sort of game that prevents them from giving any radical lead. This is a critical point we must recognise.[20]

As has been argued, being subject to the quasi-dictatorial power of global free markets and the practical imperatives of international competition, the definition of the "national interest" is necessarily extremely narrow. Indeed, as we have seen, international financial markets themselves determine and define

[20] Based on a talk given by James Robertson, former Cabinet Office policy-maker, to the Lucis Trust's Festival Week of the New Group of World Servers, December 1998.

the 'national interest' as synonymous with any policy likely to result in lower public spending, lower corporation tax, weaker trade union powers, weaker environmental regulations, etc; i.e. any policy that improves national competitiveness. As guardians of the 'national interest', political leaders of whatever party inevitably remain locked in to that narrow definition, compelled to pursue its downward spiral with ever-increasing vigour:

> **"Brown in 'green tax' climbdown.** GORDON BROWN will bow to pressure from big business today by announcing a climbdown over his plans to impose a "green" tax on industry. In his pre-Budget statement, the Chancellor will disappoint the environmental lobby by curbing the climate change levy after lobbying by Britain's bosses, who warned that it would harm productivity and cost jobs."[21]

It is no accident therefore that centre-left, Liberal or even Green parties when they gain power find themselves constrained to pursuing with even more determination the self-same policies initiated by their centre-right predecessors. It is therefore not difficult to see why politics has today become so sterile and uninteresting nor come as any surprise that in the case of Gerhard Schroeder "it's hard to see any shift from the policies of Helmut Kohl"[22]; nor that New Labour's Tony Blair is often described as the best Conservative Prime Minister since Margaret Thatcher; nor that, in referring to the new Liberal-Democrat leader, Charles Kennedy, the Financial Times cheerfully points out that "...unless he and his party learn to love economic liberalism, he will be the social democrat grandchild who never left home."[23]

---

[21] The Independent. 9th November 1999.

[22] Dieter Hundt, Trades Union Federation chief. Quoted in *The Guardian*, 17th September 1999. The same article notes: "The banks and the business lobby are happy with the chancellor, urging him to stay his course."

[23] *Financial Times*, "Leader shares his agenda with SDP founders", 21st September 1999.

Once in power, therefore, politicians of whatever party effectively have no choice but to remain confined within the policy parameters dictated by global markets and competition. Now subject to pseudo-democracy, the simple conclusion we must reach is that it no longer matters much for which party we vote. This predicament and resulting voter ambivalence consequently presents our political parties with a distinct problem: how to make themselves and their policies appear different from those of other parties when in fact the markets allow no such differentiation. How can they maintain to the electorate the illusion that they have the power to improve society, or preserve what is best in society, when the markets preclude such 'value judgements'? In a vain and desperate attempt, they are forced to employ increasingly elaborate rhetorical tricks and stunts commonly known as 'spin'. Hence the rise to prominence of the Spin Doctors.[24] For centre-left governments, attempting to reconcile their traditional social democratic values with free-market realities is resulting in the most pathetic exercises in rhetorical hair-splitting in an attempt to distract traditional left-of-centre supporters from the reality of having to submit to the liberal economic dictates of world markets:

> "French prime minister Lionel Jospin publicly distanced himself from the 'Third Way' politics of the British and German governments in a speech delivered in La Rochelle last weekend. 'We are not going in for 'social liberalism',' he promised his audience. 'Our approach is different from our friends Tony Blair and Gerhard Schroeder. We are a 'left of renewal' assembled around modern socialism.'"

But as the same article immediately goes on to reveal:

---

[24] So important have 'spin doctors' become, they often hold ministerial rank, as Peter Mandelson did following New Labour's victory at the UK 1997 General Election.

"The prime ministers's comments have been interpreted as an attempt to soothe France's old Left, which has become increasingly worried by government attempts to deregulate the economy."[25]

Since our politicians and their parties must now position themselves according to what free-market competition dictates and not necessarily to what the electorate desires they have, to a great extent, ceased to represent a mechanism through which political choice can be expressed. Instead they have become merely puppets of the quasi-dictatorship serving principally to preserve amongst the electorate the false illusion of political choice; the false illusion of democracy. Indeed, one could say that in de-regulating world markets, democracy has been hijacked and subverted by the quasi-dictatorship of global competition, its prime agents consisting of global financial markets and transnational corporations and its instruments of control being the pseudo-democratic illusion of party politics and the power and threat of competition. But this quasi-dictatorship is far more threatening than conventional dictatorships we have witnessed throughout history. For it is far more subtle and insidious and, worst of all, no one can be said to be in control of it.

The electorate too, has been infected by this paralysis. Voters are not stupid. They understand only too well what competition means. After all, they see it and are subjected to it in their daily working lives. Whilst they may not be able to precisely identify what is argued here, they certainly know that their nation cannot ignore world markets or the wider international economic environment. They know that their jobs depend to an increasing degree on their nation's competitiveness in world markets. Consequently, they are encouraged to align their votes with whichever party they perceive as most likely to maintain it. So it would be wrong to say that society submits unwillingly to global market quasi-dictatorship.

[25] *The Week.* 4th September 1999, Issue 220.

Indeed society, being infected by competition and tranquillised by pseudo-democracy, simply fails to see that it has been deprived of any real political choice. Instead, it is abandoned to the unstable and insecure forces of competition whilst believing its fate to be inevitable, unavoidable or simply, perhaps, just 'a sign of the times'.

And we should not forget the role the media plays in supporting political paralysis.[26] Its dependence on corporate advertising for continued profits as well as the fact that most of the media is itself owned by transnational corporations has left particularly those living in the USA with a media wary of reporting even world events such as the massive protests in Seattle in December 1999 against the WTO:

> "Anyone in the United States who switched on the television in the second half of Tuesday wondering what was happening in Seattle would have been little the wiser. The dozens of network and cable stations that have, in the past, shelved regular programming to show such spectacles as the OJ Simpson car chase, terrified children running out of Columbine High School, and hour upon hour of the sea off Martha's Vineyard after the Kennedy plane crash, offered viewers precisely nothing until yesterday morning. ... Viewers were given no glimpse of the street demonstrations, and no interviews with either demonstrators or delegates. ... If the disturbances in Seattle figured at all, it was in pictureless summaries lower down the bulletin. ... Media executives declined to discuss events yesterday, but it was hard to escape the impression that the absence of live coverage was, at least in part, a result of deliberate editorial judgements."[27]

So we see how society in general and politicians in particular have become subverted. We see how politicians,

---

[26] The subtle subversion of the media is well documented in *The Compassionate Revolution*. David Edwards, Green Books, 1998, chapters 2 and 3. See also *Global Spin*. Sharon Beder. Green Books, 1997.

[27] *The Independent*. 2nd December 1999.

whatever they may say prior to an election, must, once in power, act substantially in accordance with market and corporate demands often to the detriment of society and the environment. Whilst the immediate arguments for complying with those demands may seem compelling, governments, unions and members of the public alike in whatever country must wake up and urgently realise that this is a game which all must ultimately lose. While governments fail to co-operate with one another to control global markets and corporations, we are all condemned – in whatever nation we happen to find ourselves – to an on-going and profoundly un-democratic political and economic paralysis.

Paralysis it may be, but its effects are far from static. Uncontrolled competition and the world-wide spread of new technology are forces with their own powerfully negative dynamic. A dynamic which causes governments to engage not only in a progressive downgrading of social and environmental regulation in a tit-for-tat international struggle to remain attractive to transnational corporations and capital markets, but also one which forces the corporations themselves to compete fiercely against one another for market share, ever-higher short-term profits and safety from unwelcome takeovers. In this volatile and highly competitive business environment characterised by over-saturated markets the simplest way to increase profits is to cut overheads by externalising (outsourcing) every possible cost and by introducing new labour-saving technology to reduce those costs that remain:

> "A further 40,000 jobs could be in immediate danger in the banking industry because of competition from supermarkets and other newcomers to the business, according to industry estimates. ... The banking sector has been hit hard by a series of 'restructuring' exercises – some 150,000 jobs have been lost over the past seven years – but there is more to come, analysts believe. ... Mr. Batstone [of NatWest] said that before the late

Eighties a job in banking was seen as a 'job for life', but tougher competition has put paid to that. Banks wanted to replace staff with technology, he said. ... Ian Hodges, an analyst at Barclays Stockbrokers, said banks needed to encourage customers away from branches. He said: 'The challenge of the last 10 years, and perhaps the next 10, is to introduce new technology and reduce costs without alienating the existing customer base.'[28]

Under increasing competitive pressures, the harnessing of new technologies by businesses can only serve to accelerate unemployment and the inevitable social decay that goes with it:

"New technologies and the deskilling of parts of the population by inadequate education are central causes of long-term unemployment in advanced western societies. Growing income inequalities have been magnified by deregulation of the labour market and neo-liberal tax policies, but the root cause of falling wages and rising unemployment is the worldwide spread of new technology."[29]

Competition, and the drive for cost reductions it demands, is also the key driver behind environmental degradation:

"Private decision-makers operating in markets are forced by competition to find ways to reduce their costs. In so far as they fail to do so as effectively as their competitors, they will be forced out of business. One way to reduce costs is to externalize them, to organize production so that the negative impacts occur outside the market relationship. For example, when oil tankers are flushed out at sea (a common practice), the market costs of cleaning are minimized. The consequent pollution of the ocean is a social cost, but it appears nowhere in the transactions of the oil transportation industry. ...
The destruction of nature by the economic advance of human

---

[28] *The Independent.* 21st May 1999. Divisions between winners and losers in society are such that in the same newspaper, on the same date, and referring to the same item, the Business section headlines this news as "Barclays shares soar as City welcomes job cuts".

[29] *False Dawn.* John Gray. Granta Books, 1999.

beings is not a historically new process, nor is it peculiar to capitalism. The tremendously expansionary force of market activity has, however, brought environmental destruction to a global level, as evidenced by global warming and the depletion of the ozone layer. In this way of looking at things, environmental destruction is not a product of greed or human indifference to nature. It is a product of accumulation, a consequence of the way competition works through markets."[30]

Competition is, furthermore, commonly identifiable as a key barrier to reducing environmental problems at the microeconomic level of everyday experience. In my own work as supplier of filter papers to manufacturers of car air filters, for example, their production process using conventional papers can result in harmful emissions being given off to the environment. In my product portfolio, however, I can also offer a paper that can reduce these harmful emissions to a fraction of what is normally given off. But because of the special resins it contains, this paper costs about 20% more than conventional paper and my customers will not use it because the higher cost will make them uncompetitive in a global market where their customers, the major car manufacturers, can purchase anywhere in the world and can play one supplier off against another. However, because the low-emission paper represents but a fraction of the total cost of the final product, the additional cost to the consumer would be negligible. Furthermore, were all filter manufacturers obliged to use the low-emission paper, economies of scale would mean its additional cost would no longer be 20% but perhaps nearer 5%. So an improvement to the environment could be made at negligible extra cost. But due to today's intense global competition, that potential for reducing environmental impact is unnecessarily lost. I suggest that many of us working in industry could identify very many similar examples, which, if

[30] *Neo-Liberalism or Democracy?*, Arthur MacEwan, Zed Books, 1999.

taken together, would amount to a very significant reduction in environmental impact overall. So it cannot be said that solutions do not exist nor that they would cost significantly more. It is merely the cut-throat competition of a globalised free market and governments' inability to enforce higher standards that prevents us from benefiting from them.

As far as employment in the global market is concerned, one argument put in favour of free-markets is that the world-wide spread of new technology combined with the ability of corporations to shift production to lower cost countries should serve to benefit poorer countries thus leading to a narrowing of the wealth gap between rich and poor nations. Apart from the fact that most of the evidence runs counter to this, the deployment of new technology in poorer countries fails to meet the needs of the mass of their peoples. Deployed in advanced or developing countries, the effect is broadly the same: new technology simply does not require many people to operate it:

> "According to an International Labour Organisation (ILO) report, the role of TNCs in job creation is 'at best marginal'. It points out that if TNC employment is growing at all, it is 'due to acquisitions and mergers rather than to new employment opportunities'. A new TNC-owned factory may create jobs but at the cost of existing jobs in locally owned factories. A net gain of jobs may not result."[31]

Conversely, in industries where manual labour cannot be avoided, it has proved all too often to be characterised by meagerly paid exploitation.[32] Not having the necessary protective regulation and enforcement capabilities of more advanced countries, and with TNCs able to settle in almost any developing country they choose, developing nations are locked into competition with one another to attract the

[31] *Big Business, Poor Peoples.* John Madeley, Zed Books, 1999.
[32] See *The Independent*, September 1999. The paper launched the *Global Sweatshop* campaign against sweatshop labour.

TNCs and are thus subject to the same competitive forces and their consequences:

> **"Asians Feel The Heat of Competition.** Industries Become Quick To Seek Cheaper Venues. Klang, Malaysia - For more than six decades the Bata shoe factory in this port city was a source of national pride. School children came to the zinc-roofed warehouses on class trips to admire the assembly lines that produced 15,000 to 20,000 shoes a day. ... The smell of latex still hangs in the stagnant air of the warehouses here, but the assembly lines are silent. Production stopped Aug. 31, when the shoemaking operations were moved to other factories in the region. Machines were carted away and 700 workers laid off. "It's cheaper to produce the shoes in Thailand, Indonesia and Vietnam," said Kasmah Kamarudin, the human resources manager in Malaysia for Bata, a Canadian company with factories around the world.
>
> ...
>
> Thailand, starting from a lower rung than Malaysia, is trying to move up the production ladder by portraying itself as the Detroit of Southeast Asia. Ford Motor Co., General Motors Corp., Mitsubishi Motors Corp., and Toyota Motor Corp. already have auto-production plants in the country.
>
> Singapore is trying to project an image of a technology-savvy city-state...with arms wide open to an increasingly cautious crowd of foreign investors.
>
> Hong Kong ... is competing head-to-head with Singapore, trying to lure high-tech investments....
>
> Both India and the Philippines tout their ability to provide cheap back-office customer support and computer services to Western corporations.
>
> As these countries attempt to reposition themselves, rivalries have become more acute. Tensions between neighbors that were rarely publicly articulated when times were good are now out in the open.[33]

[33] International Herald Tribune. December 29th 2000.

Far from some altruistic motive to see those in poor countries improve their lot and thus narrow the gap between rich and poor, globalisation therefore merely serves as an efficient, low-cost method for TNCs to take advantage of low taxes, weak regulations and vulnerable labour whilst penetrating the economies of developing countries:

> "Rising global inequality in an era of increasing international interdependence is especially disconcerting, suggesting that globalization is generating forces that lead to the concentration instead of the dispersion of wealth. The global income distribution facts are certainly consistent with the argument that 'globalization' is simply a new term for imperialism, allowing those in the advanced countries more effective access to, control over and benefit from the world's human and natural resources."[34]

As J.K. Galbraith himself also once said:

> "Globalization is not a serious concept. We have invented it to disseminate our politics of economic entry into other countries."[35]

From the corporate point of view, however, profits must be maximised. Competition requires them to seek out the lowest possible labour costs and conditions. With fund managers watching their every move, only too ready to down-grade the stock of any "under-performing" company, failure to seek out the lowest manufacturing costs would be to lose ground against their competitors causing a reduction in profits, share price and, ultimately, the threat of an unwelcome takeover:

"Glaxo axes 3,400 jobs in move to slash costs by £370m a year. GLAXO WELLCOME, the UK's largest pharmaceutical company, is to shed 3,400 jobs, including 1,700 in Britain,

---

[34] Quoted from *Neo-Liberalism or Democracy?* Arthur MacEwan, Zed Books, 1999.
[35] Quoted from *Big Business, Poor Peoples.* John Madeley, Zed Books, 1999.

in a root-and-branch restructuring of its manufacturing operations. ...analysts said the proposed cuts, accounting for 16 per cent of the manufacturing workforce ... were higher than anticipated. Glaxo's shares closed up 20p at 1,610p. 'This is the excuse many needed to buy the shares, which have performed badly in recent weeks' said one analyst."[36]

This powerfully negative dynamic is compounded by corporations seeking shelter from competition by engaging in a cannibalistic feeding frenzy of takeovers, mergers and acquisitions. The losers, of course, are those that lose their jobs:

"**AstraZeneca cuts 1,000 research jobs.** ASTRAZENECA, the Anglo-Swedish drugs giant, is to cut 1,000 jobs in research and development, including 450 in Britain. The move comes as part of group's plan to shed 6,000 jobs by the end of 2002, following its merger earlier in the year."[37]

"**BAe axes 1,500 as Marconi merger is finalised.** AROUND 1,500 management posts are to be axed following the completion yesterday of the merger between British Aerospace and GEC's Marconi defence electronics arm to create a new company known as Baesystems. ...The job losses, which will reduce the management ranks of the new organisation to about 3,000 are part of the £275m cost savings identified when the merger was announced in January. ... Baesystems has promised to give an update on additional cost savings next spring with most analysts expecting it to achieve at least £400m. The new company will rank as the world's second-largest defence contractor..."[38]

And when two or more companies are bidding against one another to take over another company, the result is a competition to see which bidder can cut the most jobs in an effort to secure shareholder support:

[36] *The Independent.* 6th October 1999.
[37] *The Independent.* 1st December 1999.
[38] *The Independent.* 1st December 1999.

"RBS planning big cost cuts. Royal Bank of Scotland's bid for National Westminster Bank has revealed the group to be planning more aggressive cost cuts than rival bidder Bank of Scotland. The cuts - involving up to 18,000 job losses - aim to save £1.18bn over three years. Bank of Scotland said it could save £1.02bn over the same period. Cost cutting has been a key part of the battle to acquire NatWest..."[39]

Whilst competition is held to be beneficial to consumers by resulting in lower prices, the logic of the global market inevitably results in the opposite effect. For the drive for competitive advantage, cost reductions and survival results not in enhanced competition but in the opposite: corporate consolidation. As a consequence, governments have established all manner of so-called 'competition regulators' in an attempt to curb the worst excesses of corporate mergers. But a globalised free-market forces governments to view mergers and acquisitions in a global context, often allowing further consolidation at the expense of the public interest:

"New media giant vows to take on Murdoch. Carlton Communications and United News and Media confirmed a £7.8bn merger yesterday that will turn them into Britain's largest media company. ...

The combined company is so big that it will break the legal limit that does not allow any one company to take more than 25 per cent of television advertising revenues. However, many stock analysts believe that the OFT [Office of Fair Trading] may allow the deal to go ahead anyway. The watchdog is already conducting a review of the 25 per cent limit, which was imposed in 1994. Since then, there has been considerable pressure to allow media companies to consolidate in order to compete effectively in the digital age, and to take advantage of global markets. ...

City speculation has now turned to the possibility of yet more consolidation,..."[40]

[39] *Financial Times.* 30th November 1999.

Whether it is corporate consolidation or the introduction of new technology, therefore, the inevitable result of inadequately regulated competition is ever-increasing unemployment accompanied by consequent social or environmental decay and a concentration of economic power in ever-fewer hands.

Some hold out the hope that TNCs can be influenced towards more socially and environmentally responsible behaviour. But this is to misunderstand both the legal and business framework within which corporations operate. Company law demands that directors must always "act in the best interests of the company". (I am a company director, so I know.) Since "interests" can ultimately be measured only in monetary terms, it amounts to a legal obligation to maximise profits paying minimum regard to any (usually weak) social or environmental regulations. In a business environment where competitors are only too ready to step in where environmentally or socially conscious companies might hesitate, not only would self-restraint be futile, it would be damaging for any company exercising it. Furthermore, directors of such companies would place themselves at risk of legal action by shareholders for failing to "act in the best interests of the company." Any influence that might be brought to bear on corporations can therefore only result in token and cosmetic actions designed merely to promote a benign yet false public image. Unless company law around the world is both adjusted and combined with effective means of enforcement no tangible improvement to the environment or to the corporate role in society can be expected.

Similarly, we should also not be lulled into a false sense of security by the often genuine use by some corporations of "Social and Ethical Accounting, Auditing and Reporting" (SEAAR) or other similar procedures. Whilst these may assist

---

[40] *The Independent.* 27th November 1999.

in improving a corporation's attitude and behaviour to social and environmental issues, they fail to address the dynamics of competition, particularly with respect to job losses. As a member of one corporation leading in SEAAR pointed out:

> "Still questions abound. For example, what does fair treatment of workers really mean? Are layoffs fair? And if they are not fair, can anyone really expect such fairness? Is there a difference between, on the one hand, two large, profitable banks merging and eliminating thousands of jobs and, on the other hand, a manufacturing business laying off workers in response to slow sales?"[41]

Indeed, in the Age of Competition, these *are* the crucial questions; questions which new methods of 'accounting' have yet to properly answer and upon which they remain eerily silent. That the procedures followed by such corporations to make employees redundant may be 'fair' or 'ethical' and that there may have been no alternative is therefore of little comfort, particularly to those who, having lost their jobs, no longer form part of the corporation's 'stakeholders'. (Furthermore, I suggest that the use of the words 'social' and 'ethical' imply a far wider and grander scope of application than these procedures merit and is therefore prone to mislead the public as well as investors. The less grand and simpler title of 'Stakeholder Accounting' might perhaps be more appropriate.)

In conclusion, therefore, whilst competition is held to be the engine of innovation and lower prices for consumers, we must now wake up to its less obvious and highly dangerous effects; effects which the global free market is fast demonstrating far outweigh those much-trumpeted benefits. Indeed, it is surely high time that the religion of competition which purports to have exclusively positive effects was well and truly debunked. In the absence of international regulation of world

[41] Alan Parker, Ben & Jerry's Homemade, Inc. quoted from *Building Corporate AccountAbility*, Earthscan Publications Ltd., 1997.

markets and TNCs, surely we must realise that we are all being forced to play a dangerous game that no one is in control of and no one can be held responsible for. Neither, under pseudo-democracy, is there any evident exit from it. We are all of us caught in a vicious circle in which there can ultimately be no long-term winners and from which there is ordinarily no way out.

Whilst the vicious circle continues there are, of course, big short term winners: shareholders and the overpaid corporate executives who do their bidding. It should therefore come as no surprise that the gap between rich and poor is growing at an alarming rate:

> "**The rich are still getting richer.** Despite last year's economic panic, the world's millionaires continued to get richer. The combined wealth of the six million wealthiest people reached $21.6 thousand billion (£13.5 thousand billion), up by 12 per cent over last year and it is likely to grow by 9 per cent over the next five years, according to research conducted by Merrill Lynch, the investment bank, and Gemini Consulting, a management consultancy."[42]

> "**UK bosses get 17% pay rises.** CHIEF EXECUTIVES at the UK's 100 largest companies saw their pay packages rise by 17.6 per cent on average in the last financial year, according to a survey published today by the pay research company Incomes Data Services. The report ... finds that "even annual bonus payments" showed weak links with companies' performance and profits ..."[43]

In the longer term, however, weakening social cohesion resulting from the widening gap between rich and poor fuelled by increasing unemployment is already manifesting itself in the growing power of xenophobic groups and far-right political parties. With centre-right parties largely redundant and soulless centre-left parties pandering to market and

[42] *The Independent.* 18th May 1999.
[43] *The Independent.* 27th October 1999.

corporate whims, evidence of a resort to far-right political parties is already mounting and we should hardly need reminding of its ultimate consequences:

"The tendency has long been apparent to anyone with the eyes to see it. The wave of xenophobia among the European and American population is an unmistakable sign that politics has for years had to take into account. Refugees and immigrants have had their human rights considerably curtailed through ever harsher laws and surveillance in nearly every European country as well as in the United States. ...

The next round of exclusions is directed against economically weak groups in society: receivers of income support, the jobless and disabled, the young. These people experience more and more the withdrawal of support or fellow-feeling on the part of those who are still 'winners'. Themselves threatened with relegation, peaceful middle-class citizens turn into prosperity chauvinists who are no longer willing to pay for losers in the game of world-market roulette."[44]

"**Victory for the far right**: Jorg Haider, the populist far-right politician who has expressed his admiration for Hitler, won a major victory in last weekend's regional election in the southern state of Carinthia. Haider's Freedom Party took more than 42% of the vote, well ahead of Austria's ruling party, the Social Democrats, with only 30%. It is the first time the party has won a majority in any of Austria's nine states, and should ensure that Haider is named Governor of Carinthia, the post from which he had to resign in 1991 after praising Hitler."[45]

"**Neo-Nazi violence in Sweden**: Sweden was in a state of shock last week following two separate car bomb explosions. ... The bombs have caused bewilderment in Sweden, widely regarded as the most liberal society in Europe. Increased immigration and the effects of economic recession have stimulated a burgeoning neo-Nazi movement in Sweden."[46]

[44] *The Global Trap.* Martin & Schumann. Zed Books 1997.
[45] *The Week.* 13th March 1999. Issue 195

"Far-right's success will end Swiss consensus. Switzerland's cosy democracy was jolted at the weekend as a far-right party made spectacular electoral gains... For the moment, Mr Blocher's triumph can be ignored, but such a strategy goes against the Swiss tradition of consensus government."[47]

"Hague defies calls to cool down race row. William Hague fuelled the political debate over race last night by warning that Britain faced a "massive influx of bogus asylum-seekers",... the Tory leader made clear the controversial issue would remain a central plank in his party's campaigning."[48]

"Schroeder gets a mauling at polls. Germany's ruling Social Democrats suffered catastrophic losses in two key regional elections yesterday... Mr. Schroeder's party lost the western state of Saarland to the oppostion..., and in the eastern state of Brandenburg the SPD's share of the vote collapsed by 15 percentage points,... The neo-Nazis of the German People's Union, based in Munich, entered Brandenburg's state parliament for the first time with a vote of 5.2%. ... Mr. Schroeder's bad day was compounded by the fact that in both states the Greens, his junior coalition partner, failed to surmount the 5% hurdle required to enter parliament."[49]

And we would be foolish to believe that such tendencies will remain safely under wraps within the confines of a newly strengthened EU. Since free financial markets and competition are truly global phenomena, so too is the growing popularity of the new far-right:

"Tokyo elects anti-Western extremist. The dark side of Japan's imperial past has resurfaced, says Toru Hayano [of *Asahi Shimbun*]. The election of the ultra-right-wing Shintaro Ishihara as mayor of Tokyo is a worrying sign that voters are disillusioned with the political stalemate that has crippled

[46] *The Week*. 10th July 1999. Issue 212.
[47] *The Independent*, 26th October 1999.
[48] *The Independent*, 11th May 2000.
[49] *The Guardian*. 6th September 1999.

national politics. In despair, they are turning to authoritarian figures like Ishihara who promise to clean up corruption and end the cronyism which is endemic in Japanese government. But behind his smooth promises are some unsavoury beliefs, such as a refusal to accept Japan's responsibility for the Rape of Nanking, or the existence of Korean 'comfort women'. He is violently anti-American and anti-Nato."[50]

As if the social consequences of continued runaway competition were not worrying enough, the competition between nation states in pursuit of their respective 'national interests' similarly heralds dire environmental and human consequences:

> "Researchers at several universities say that climate change can only be halted by a 70 per cent cut in greenhouse gas emissions… And if it is not halted, they warn, there could be catastrophic global consequences, including sharp rises in drought and famine, the spread of disease and the death of huge areas of tropical forest. So far, though, there is little prospect of such a drastic cut. At the Kyoto Summit two years ago, the industrialised world agreed to reduce emissions by five per cent by 2010, and even that target has run into problems. The US - which has four per cent of the world's population but produces 20 per cent of its pollution - shows little sign of co-operating with the Kyoto target…"[51]

GLOBAL SIMULTANEOUS IMPLEMENTATION: FANTASY OR NECESSITY?

With international politics now irrevocably paralysed by pseudo-democracy and with corporations left to cause social and environmental havoc in the name of maintaining their competitiveness, it is indeed difficult to see any way out of

[50] *The Week*. 1st May 1999.
[51] *The Week*. 15th April 2000.

this predicament; a predicament which, both practically and theoretically, can perhaps best be understood in terms of competition having become unshackled from cooperation. For if it is to be beneficial and fair, competition must always occur within a framework of a universally appropriate, equitable and respected set of rules and the global economy is surely no exception. Cooperation between all the participants in the competition or game is needed both to define those rules and to respect and police them. Be it a children's game, an olympic athletics race or trade in the world economy, competition must always be *held subordinate* to cooperation. If it is not, it quickly gets out of control and under such circumstances, as any parent knows, even a children's game can quickly lead to a small war. Since no transnational institution nor any comprehensive association of nations exists capable of enforcing appropriate rules upon globally mobile capital and TNCs, it can truly be said that today those key elements of economic competition have become disembedded from cooperation and are now running out of control.

Interestingly, there does exist one institution having supra-national authority in trade matters, that being the World Trade Organisation (WTO). Ironically, however, far from imposing appropriate regulations on the free movement of capital and TNCs which would restore a large measure of economic control to nation states, the prime function of the WTO's remit of trade liberalisation is to *preserve* their free movement. After all, 'liberalisation' is the opposite of 'regulation'. The contradiction between the free movement of capital and TNCs on one hand, and democracy on the other, can thus clearly be seen. Preserving their power over nation states simply serves to preserve the subversion of democracy. That the leaders of nation states not only fail to recognise this but actually *support* the unrestricted movement of capital and corporations, i.e. the key factors undermining their own power base and thus their own existence, serves to illuminate the current very poor state of both politics and democracy. But I believe it is generally true to say that this state of affairs is not the result of an 'evil conspiracy' on the part of transnational corporations, market traders or fund managers but merely the natural consequence of competition having become unshackled from cooperation. After all, in the case of corporations, their evolution to becoming transnational has been a function of ever-greater size driven by the need for increased profits and market share in an increasingly competitive environment; in the case of the markets, on the other hand, the cause was a deliberate, but foolhardy policy of deregulation on the part of politicians in the belief that greater prosperity would result. Evil conspiracy or not, the inability of politicians to regain control leaves them little option but to accept this situation while claiming its effects to be 'natural' or 'inevitable'.

> Former U.S. President Bill Clinton: "Globalization is not a policy choice, it is a fact."
> UK Prime Minister Tony Blair: Globalisation is "irreversible and irresistible."[52]

Politicians' acceptance of the free market and globalisation as 'inevitable' or 'natural' is both interesting and highly significant because it reveals what could be called 'the mind-set of competition'; a mind-set which represents nothing less than the terms of reference or framework within which the minds of politicians, the leaders of the multi-lateral institutions (WTO, IMF, WB) and the economists who support them work. It therefore subconsciously determines the parameters, preconceptions and scope within which all their thoughts and decisions must necessarily be framed. This mind-set amounts

---

[52] "Globalization is not a policy choice, it is a fact." – Bill Clinton, Speech to the WTO, 18th May 1998. Globalization is "irreversible and irresistible" – Tony Blair, Speech to the WTO, 19th May 1998.

to a one-demensional, myopic and ultimately flawed under-standing of competition itself. For it sees competition as exclusively beneficial whilst totally failing to see or recognise its destructive side. Now this is highly significant because, if you are a politician, it necessarily leads to a flawed thought-process which runs something like this: "Globalisation is inevitable and so is the free-market because there is, in any case, no way to stop it – in fact it's probably natural anyway. The reality of the global market is global competition. So we must compete. And the better we compete, the richer we become. Since getting rich is good (and it will win us votes), so competition must be good. And to have its full effect, com-petition must be enforced consistently on a world-wide basis if we are all to become richer. So we must establish and support a supra-national 'competition-enforcer' to do so." Hence the establishment of the WTO.

In the light of the loss of control over the global economy on the part of national governments, it is not quite correct to see the WTO, as many do, as the cause and focus of our global ills. After all, financial market deregula-tion and the ability of TNCs to move production across national borders are both phenomena which clearly pre-date the establishment of the WTO. But having unwitting-ly lost control over the global economy and then found themselves abandoned both to its competitive forces and mind-set, the only response national governments could make was to ensure that competition exerted its 'inevitable' force more rigorously, mechanistically and 'fairly' by estab-lishing the WTO. We should, therefore, more properly regard the WTO as a *symptom* of the absence of political control over the global economy rather than its cause. It is therefore the lack of control over globally mobile capital and corporations which should instead represent the true focus of our attention.

Similarly, we should also ask ourselves whether it is really correct to see the International Monetary Fund (IMF) as being in control of the global financial system. Although its directors doubtless see themselves as such, the IMF is largely the creature of the G-7 group of most powerful nations who, as we have seen, are themselves incapable of re-imposing any meaningful re-regulation on internationally mobile capital and corporations. So what chance the IMF? It should therefore not surprise us that their prescriptions for introducing economic stability restrict themselves to 'soft' measures such as 'greater transparency' or 'enhanced surveillance to provide improved "early warning" of imminent financial crises' and so on.

Furthermore, the flawed acceptance by politicians and the multi-lateral institutions of global competition as inevitable and exclusively beneficial can never lead to policies that are appropriate. For as we have seen, competition also has a highly destructive side which must be taken in to account. But being subject to the 'mind-set of competition' and therefore blind to that destructive side, our political leaders and the multi-lateral institutions are of course bound to prescribe yet *more* competition (i.e. more 'Structural Adjustment', more privatisation, more cuts in tax and public services, etc.) as the cure to those destructive effects and not less. In this way they will tend to exacerbate global poverty still further whilst honestly – but wrongly - believing they are helping to reduce it.

By contrast, however, we should also be clear that destructive competition is not just the unacceptable symptom of global free trade. It is equally the unacceptable feature of protectionism so often characterised by a competitive, tit-for-tat raising of national trade barriers so often cited by free-marketeers as the cause of previous world wars. Indeed, no single doctrine, be it global free-trade or global protectionism, can offer an answer to our problems. Nor can economic justice or environmental and employment security be fostered within a framework of unfettered competition of either variety. After all, competition is not about justice or security - it's about *winning*. As the inevitable symptom of both hitherto available paradigms, it shouldn't be too difficult to deduce that destructive competition *itself* represents the underlying problem.

Far from a glorious ride to global prosperity, therefore, "we stand on the brink not of the era of plenty that free-marketeers project, but a tragic epoch, in which anarchic market forces and shrinking natural resources drag sovereign states into ever more dangerous rivalries. ... The likelihood must be that the *laissez-faire* regime will not be reformed. Instead it will fracture and fragment, as mounting scarcities of resources and conflicts of interest among the world's great powers make international cooperation ever more difficult. A deepening international anarchy is the human prospect."[53]

But fully in the face of this desperate state of affairs, in this book I shall argue not only that widespread, if not universal cooperation between nation states is feasible but that such an approach also offers an infinitely more effective means of addressing our problems; a means based on a range of policies implemented co-operatively by all nations simultaneously. Furthermore, not only will this book argue such a far-reaching vision to be perfectly compatible within the framework of current world politics, it will outline a feasible means of achieving it. Whilst many readers may throw their hands up in ridicule at this proposition, in the light of the circumstances described above, surely the question is not how realistic or otherwise such a proposal might be, but *what other choice do the people of the world have* – be they in advanced, developing or non-industrial countries – if they are to free themselves from the domination of financial markets or, for that matter, from any other markets that force nations to

---

[53] *False Dawn*. John Gray. Granta Books, 1998.

compete with one another to the detriment of their societies? Such is the 'golden' merry-go-round the world has decided to get on to: now it is spinning so fast no nation alone is able to get off (unless it is forcibly ejected by the market itself). Nor would any nation or group of nations be capable of slowing it down. Indeed if it were not so destructive to mankind, the idea of nations having embarked upon a merry-go-round from which they now find they are unable to disembark would be almost laughable. Amusing as the thought may be, we should take seriously the perfectly logical solution. There remains, therefore, only one possible way to both slow and control the merry-go-round and to address our two world problems: a global and simultaneous one in which all nations act together. Indeed, in a globally competitive context, global simultaneous action now remains the only method of escaping that vicious circle and of shifting opinion and policy away from free-market fundamentalism.[54]

Even if re-regulation of free financial markets and corporations were achieved - and achieved it must be if we are to restore genuine democracy and avoid the catastrophic consequences of a move to the far-right – we will continue to be faced by our two world problems of achieving Right Livelihood and Right Human Relations: the 'ugly sisters' that simply refuse to go away. How much longer are we going to go on denying their existence, continually allowing ourselves to be hoodwinked by attractive but deadly golden merry-go-rounds?[55] World consciousness calls ever louder to all humanity to see the futility of running away from them.

---

[54] To underline the argument for the necessity of widespread if not global simultaneous action, in adopting the Tobin Tax in May/June 1999, the resolution of the Canadian Parliament states that it should only be enacted "in concert with the international community".

[55] Denial of responsibility is a common psychological phenomenon with often serious consequences. See *The Road Less Traveled*. M. Scott Peck. Arrow, 1990. Pages 40-44.

Surely we cannot allow the survivors of a Third World War or a descent into widespread civil unrest and rebel warfare to look back and identify the 1990s as the decade in which the writing was on the wall but nobody took action. For it is precisely at such moments in history that the course of world events can be influenced – indeed *must* be influenced – if disasters such as the two world wars of last century are to be averted. Many might think such horrors cannot possibly happen again but the inequalities, social exclusion and growing xenophobia that we see today existed in the build-up to those horrors and we ignore them at our peril. The strangle-hold that global free markets now exert over domestic national politics in whatever country has effectively disabled governments of whatever party from pursuing policies to protect labour, the environment or the poor. In these circumstances it is hardly surprising that weakening social cohesion is today accompanied by the rise of the far right. In the light of these obvious warning signs, do we really want to be remembered as the generation that ignored those dire warnings because it was too busy fixing the millennium computer bug?

Our two world problems are human problems that cannot be escaped; problems which can only be recognised and confronted if we and our children are to survive. We must now accept them and deal with them before it is too late. To deal with them we must accept or 'own' them and then take responsibility for solving them. To own them, we must turn our backs on Chaos and strive for Community. To do so, we must find the courage to enter the era of Emptiness: the elusive bridge that will take us from Chaos towards Community. In the Age of Competition, that bridge may appear more elusive than ever, but as we shall see, it can be found.

4. From Competition to Co-operation

"What at this moment appears to prevent world unity and keeps the United Nations from arriving at those necessary settlements which the man in the street is so eagerly awaiting? The answer is not hard to find and involves all nations: nationalism, capitalism, competition, blind stupid greed."[1]

So the world remains caught in the seemingly irrevocable grip of competitive chaos even though its consciousness is beginning to yearn for the era of emptiness. How can we get there? Can the nation state still offer any hope in the age of global capital? Can we look to the United Nations or to larger blocks of nation states such as the European Union to help or find a way out?

THE UNITED NATIONS

The purposes of the UN are "to maintain international peace and security, to develop friendly relations among nations, to achieve international co-operation in solving problems, and to act as a centre for harmonising collective action. These purposes are action loaded. They only bear fruit if 'collective measures' are appropriate and effective. The UN is to serve three interrelated functions: namely, to be a forum for discussion and decision, to meet as a syndicate for action, employing non-forcible measures to improve the

[1] *Problems of Humanity.* Alice A. Bailey. Lucis Publishing Co, 1947.

world, and to be a missionary centre appealing to moral values and standards higher than those generally prevailing in international relations."[2]

The crucial factor, however, remains that of national sovereignty. The purposes of the UN in general, and its ability to resolve our two world problems in particular, are possible only insofar as nation states would be prepared to submit or relinquish their sovereignty to the UN thus allowing the UN to impose the necessary reforms worldwide (assuming it knew what reforms were required). The obstacle, however, is article 2:1 of the UN Charter which allows for no relinquishing of national sovereignty. Indeed, "the United Nations is not constituted to maintain or wield an adequate supranational police force in the event that a nation-state commits an illegal or immoral act. It is not just a question of personnel and weaponry; it does not have the authority to pursue such a course of action. But the UN is not so constituted precisely because its member nation-states have not wanted it to be. They have been unwilling to relinquish their own authority. In fact, supranational government is incompatible with the nation-state system."[3]

Whilst there is neither democratic representation for civil society in the form of an elected world parliament within the UN organisation which would confer upon the UN the authority to compel member states to comply, the UN can have no independent authority over its members and therefore remains impotent when it comes to protecting the world's environments and peoples. Whilst it doubtless carries out much essential work, the UN is largely hamstrung (through no fault of its own) by the unwillingness of its member states to relinquish their sovereignty. Equally, looking at the same issue from the point of view of member nations,

[2] *The United Nations in the Contemporary World*. David Whittaker. Routledge, 1997.
[3] *The Different Drum*. M. Scott Peck. Arrow, 1990.

without direct civil society representation at the UN in the form of an elected world parliament, member states have no legitimate grounds upon which a relinquishing of their sovereignty could be justified.[4] In short, we have what appears to be a classic, insoluble situation. In the meantime the UN seems doomed to remain merely a higher reflection of the competitive behaviour of its member states:

> "The rhetoric that ornaments conferences and conventions ritually calls for a new global ethic, but the reality at the negotiating tables suggests a different logic. There, for the most part, one sees diplomats engaged in the familiar game of accumulating advantages for their countries, eager to out-manoeuvre their opponents, shrewdly tailoring environmental concerns to the interests dictated by their particular nation's economic position. Their parameters of action are bounded by the need to extend their nation's space for 'development'; in their hands environmental concerns turn into bargaining chips in the struggle of interests. In that respect, the thrust of UNCED's negotiations was no different from the thrust of previous negotiations about the Law of the Sea, the Antarctic, or the Montreal protocol on the reduction of CFCs. Forthcoming negotiations on climate, animal protection or biodiversity are unlikely to be any different."[5]

In terms of the resolution of our two world problems, therefore, it seems the UN can never fulfil any more worthwhile function than providing a forum for communication, though this is not to be undervalued.

As far as the prospects for reform of the UN are concerned, "two things about reform are virtually certain. First, the major

---

[4] The lack of democratic civil society representation at the UN and the consequent absence of the necessary justification for the ceding of national sovereignty to it has, however, not prevented governments from ceding sovereignty to other global institutions such as the WTO.

[5] *Planet Dialectics - Explorations in Environment and Development.* Wolfgang Sachs, Zed Books, 1999.

powers sitting comfortably in the privilege of the Security Council reveal marked reservations about any reform thought damaging to their status and interests. ... Second, from a wider perspective, UN reforms can only be rated as failing or succeeding if the attitudes of UN member states change."[5] Furthermore, with regard to the issue of sustainability, "the position several years after Rio appears to be that while the majority of countries accept the frequently proclaimed tenets of sustainability and would like to see them realised they do not quite see how the precepts are to become operable in the near future given the constraints of their own poor leverage and the likely restraints, qualifications and evasions that vested interests (mainly among the rich) are likely to resort to."[6]

In conclusion therefore, the UN is incapable of offering a way out of our current predicament and its inability to take an independent stance has too often left it stranded in the doldrums of international affairs allowing some of its bodies to be easily co-opted to corporate ends:

> "...the well-respected United Nations Development Programme (UNDP) has begun a new programme of co-operation with some of the world's most destructive corporations - all in the name of 'developing' the Third World. The joint programme is called the 'Global Sustainable Development Facility (GSDF) - 2B2M: 2 Billion People to the Market by 2020. So far, 16 multinational corporations are paying $50,000 each to sign on as sponsors. ... The purpose of the 2B2M/GSDF project, in the UNDP's own words, is to 'create sustainable economic growth and allow the private sector to prosper through the inclusion of two billion new people in the global market economy'."[7]

> "In the early 1990s some Western governments were intent on closing down UNCTAD [the United Nations Conference on

---

[6] *The United Nations in the Contemporary World.* David Whittaker. Routledge, 1997.
[7] From an article by Joshua Karliner appearing in *The Ecologist*, August/September 1999.

Trade and Development whose mandate was to help poor countries with their trade and development efforts] unless changes were made. The organisation was even given some perks, such as taking over responsibility for running the UN Commission on Transnational Corporations from the defunct UNCTC. Following the setting up of the World Trade Organisation in 1994, Western leaders recommended that UNCTAD's role be reviewed; this review effectively took place at the ninth UNCTAD conference in 1996. UNCTAD remains in business although with a very different mandate. Its chief task now seems to be one of smoothing the path for TNC investment in developing countries."[8]

But in the face of UN impotence, the need for global governance remains urgent. Jeff Gates points out that:

"The notions of ecosphere and biosphere reflect the relatively recent admission that just as by-products of economic activity cross the borders of politically sovereign nations, so too must efforts to deal with them. However, short of a world government or the emergence of strengthened and well-funded international institutions (such as the United Nations), mankind lacks both an institutional structure and a comprehensive economic theory capable of addressing today's environmental challenges."[9]

It could therefore be said that whilst the UN possesses the *mechanics* required for co-operation, until the issues of national sovereignty and democratic civil society representation are addressed, it can never provide the necessary *dynamics*.

THE NATION STATE

Given the inability of the UN or other international fora to assist us, a further question we should perhaps ask is whether nation states are themselves capable *in principle* of effecting

[8] *Big Business - Poor Peoples.* John Madeley, Zed Books Ltd, 1999.
[9] *The Ownership Solution.* Jeff Gates. Penguin Press, 1998.

reforms even if they were to act in concert. The erosion of the powers of the state to protect social cohesion in the face of global free capital flows has brought some to question whether capital has perhaps finally outgrown democracy and can no longer be controlled by it. There are generally two factions within the body of people that hold this view.

Firstly there are the free-market fundamentalists who have always supported the idea of global free markets: those such as Kenichi Ohmae who seem to believe the function of the nation state is to act merely as a kind of 'local authority', submitting itself to the needs of corporations to carry on their global or international businesses. This category could also include economists such as Michael Porter who appear to celebrate competition as if it were a magical cure for all problems:

> "One unchanging certainty, however, is that competition will continue to be both evolving, unsettling, and the source of much of our prosperity. If this collection [of essays] could convey only one message, I would want it to be a sense of the staggering power of competition to make things better - both for companies and for society."[10]

Or even those supposedly enlightened and well-meaning politicians such as former U.S. Vice President, Al Gore, who still cling to the notion that somehow free markets can bring solutions:

> "As the world's leading exemplar of free market economics, the United States has a special obligation to discover effective ways of using the power of market forces to help save the global environment."[11]

---

[10] *On Competition*. Michael E. Porter et al. Harvard Business Review, 1998. Porter has also written *The Competitive Advantage of Nations* which rather underlines the current preoccupation of nation states to compete effectively with one another. Even Porter, however, is starting to warn governments of the dangers of corporate consolidation. See *The Sunday Times*, 26th September 1999.

[11] *Earth in the Balance*. Al Gore. Earthscan Publications Ltd, 1992.

That voyage of discovery is likely, I suggest, to prove entirely fruitless.

Secondly there are those who are suffering from the psychology of helplessness: those who assume nothing can be done so it won't be done. This group is probably even more dangerous than its fundamentalist partners. In *The Different Drum*, written before the end of the Cold War, M. Scott Peck speaks about the psychology of helplessness during the arms race. A passage is quoted below substituting only the words "arms race" with " the global free market":

> "The root of helplessness that I believe to be the strongest is ignorance or lack of knowledge. People feel most helpless in the face of [the global free market], I suspect, simply because they do not understand it. And because they do not understand it, they cannot see the way out. It is not well understood by most psychologists and theologians because they lack the knowledge of politics and economics. Worst of all, it is even less understood by politicians and business people who are primarily "in charge" of it because they don't understand the psychology or theology involved. And, finally, none of them has much understanding because most of them lack the knowledge of community."[12]

Nevertheless, what we must first understand is that capitalism has an 'Achilles heel': that capitalism in fact depends upon the nation state:

> "Capitalist society is founded on the creation of saleable commodities, from which profits can be realised. Both the creation of the commodities and their sale for profit involve marketplace transactions....
> There must be an institution which can create rules of contract compliance that hold for all contracts entered into within the territory where that law holds; it must also have the power to hear cases against accused malefactors and impose

---

[12] *The Different Drum*. M. Scott Peck. Arrow, 1990.

punishments if the accusations are found to be valid. That institution, with sovereign power over the population of a defined territory, is the state."[13]

Indeed, as John Gray points out:

"Sovereign states are not going to become obsolete. They will remain decisive mediating structures which multinational corporations compete to control. This pivotal role of sovereign states makes non-sense of the claims of the hyperglobalists, business utopians and populists who maintain that multinationals have supplanted sovereign states as the real rulers of the world. It explains why global markets seek leverage over states and why they cannot ignore them. It illuminates the narrow margin in which governments can act to help their citizens control economic risk. This protective function of states is likely to expand, as citizens demand shelter from the anarchy of global capitalism."[14]

This pivotal role of nation states means that political leaders could start to implement change but only if they both saw the need and could find a practical method of doing so:

"States have immense powers to act, economically, militarily, politically and ideologically. Those powers present those controlling the state apparatus with myriad opportunities. Which opportunities they perceive and act upon, and why, is a matter of local determination, reflecting both the immediate context of any decision-making and the cultural matrix within which that is set."[15]

In an age of globally mobile capital and corporations the restoration of the state's legitimacy as the democratically elected authority over its people depends, however, on its ability to act in concert with other states to control the forces of global free markets which have eroded that legitimacy.

[13] *Nature, State and Economy*. Ronald K. Johnston. John Wiley & Sons Ltd, 1996.
[14] *False Dawn*. John Gray. Granta Books, 1998.
[15] *Nature, State & Economy*. Ronald K. Johnston. John Wiley & Sons Ltd, 1996.

Today the nation state can only do so through widespread, if not universal, co-operation with other nation states.

THE EUROPEAN UNION

From the global perspective of free markets and international competition, the formation of the European Union by dint of its importance in world markets and its capacity for economic self-sufficiency is often thought to offer a safe haven in which the traditional European social market model can once again flourish in spite of the forces of global competition. Indeed, like the rapid corporate consolidation that characterises the global free market, the drive to ever-greater European political and economic integration can, to a large extent, also be seen as a consequence of global competition. But the EU provides, in all likelihood, merely a temporary respite for its member states against those forces and their detrimental effects on employment and social cohesion. The logic of international competition demands that protection for EU member states cannot last long against the competitive pressures from other economies such as China or the USA whose businesses do not carry the same environmental or social costs. Ultimately the EU as a block will be forced to compete head-on against NAFTA, Japan, China and the other economies of the Far East: a contest which by dint of higher taxation and the much higher costs its businesses have to bear, it is ill-equipped to win. Indeed, one can already identify this inherent weakness with respect to tax harmonisation, for example. The failure to introduce a Europe-wide tax on savings, the so-called 'Withholding Tax', because of Britain's fear of jobs fleeing the City of London for New York or elsewhere demonstrates that the EU cannot ignore either the rest of the world or the mobility of the markets:

"Last night the [EU] summit agreed a face-saving formula under which the EU will set up a working group to try to break the deadlock... Mr. Blair and the Chancellor, Gordon Brown, hailed the review as a sign that Britain was winning the argument that tax evasion had to be tackled on a world-wide basis."[16]

Perhaps the early months of the single European currency, the Euro, best demonstrate the power of the markets to impose their will regardless of the desires of either citizens or politicians. Since its launch, the market consistently down-valued the Euro principally as a result of what it saw as underlying 'structural weaknesses' in euro-zone economies: high public spending, generous welfare provision, protected labour markets, etc. The response to the verdict of the markets was therefore entirely predictable:

"In Brussels, a joint statement by ministers expressed concern at the euro's plight and promised to push through reforms to their economies to make them more competitive."[17]

As Mr. Klaus-Dieter Kuehbacher, the Bundesbank council member, reluctantly conceded:

"There is nothing left for Europe than to push ahead with structural reforms".[18]

Making good that promise to conform to market demands was then not long in following:

"Chancellor Gerhard Schroeder yesterday pulled off a stunning victory on tax reform, paving the way for a radical restructuring of Germany's corporate landscape. ... Economists said passage of the tax reforms marked a watershed because Germany had gained a reputation in the 1990s as a high-tax, low-growth and institutionally rigid society. The effect could

---

[16] *The Independent.* 11th December 1999.
[17] *The Times.* 9th May 2000.
[18] *The Financial Times.* 10th May 2000.

be that international investors see the euro-zone in a more positive light, leading to higher direct and portfolio investment and causing the euro to emerge from its prolonged period of weakness on foreign exchange markets. ... Now that the two chambers of parliament have approved the tax package, Germany can portray itself more credibly as a proponent of economic reform. This may encourage other euro-zone countries, notably France and Italy, to go down the German route stimulating competition among national tax policies and creating better opportunities for business."[19]

Whilst these deregulatory reforms are portrayed as benefiting the German economy by making it more competitive, the adverse effects on German society and environment are likely to mirror what has already happened in countries like the UK during the 1980s: corporate consolidation and job losses, failing public services, increased poverty, a widening gap between rich and poor, an increasing recourse to far-right political parties, etc. Furthermore, when Germany's reforms have taken full effect and have spread to other euro-zone economies, the UK, the USA and possibly other economies will be forced to respond in a bid to maintain their own 'competitiveness' and attractiveness to internationally mobile capital by making yet more cuts in their own levels of corporate taxation and public spending. And so the vicious circle of competition continues.

In conclusion, therefore, it seems clear that the options open to the EU are little different from those available to individual nation states. The need for global co-operation as a means of restoring control over world markets and corporations thus remains paramount. Furthermore, those in charge of nation states, our political leaders, must first perceive the need to regain control before they can consider what action might be appropriate.

[19] *The Financial Times*. 15/16th July 2000.

FIGHTING OVER SANDWICHES

In the context of existing institutions being unable to assist us, and being subject now to the quasi-dictatorship of the markets and of worldwide competition, indeed how can we, the individual voters in the growing number of so-called democratic states around the world, overcome this seemingly intractable situation? Indeed, how can we make any difference at all when pseudo-democracy renders our votes meaningless and the UN or EU hold out little hope of reforming our economic system, or questioning blind faith in economic growth? If the only way out of quasi-dictatorship is for all nations to act together, how could we possibly get them to co-operate when they are all much more preoccupied with competing against one another? How on earth, then, can there be any chance of bringing them to implement profound measures that address our two world problems?

To answer these questions, we need to go back to basics – to our childhoods - in order to re-learn the lesson of reconciliation: the lesson that teaches us how we can make the vital transition from competition to co-operation. It is a lesson each of us learnt in the playground but which, in the Age of Competition, a whole generation around the world seems to have forgotten.

Let us imagine, therefore, that we are back in the school playground and we observe four or five boys fighting over a packet of sandwiches which, if they co-operated with one another, they could perfectly easily share. If one or two of them opt out of the fight, they deny themselves access to the sandwiches and go hungry, leaving the other two to fight it out with one boy ending up with all of them (if they are not rendered inedible in the scuffle). To maintain the chance of a sandwich, all must therefore continue fighting. As we look on, in the end we see that they do nevertheless manage to stop fighting and go off happily to share the sandwiches. Let's see how they do it.

The punches are flying right, left and centre. None of the boys looks like they have any intention of giving up. After some minutes and a few bruises, however, one of the boys, David, says: "Look guys", - whilst giving one or more of them another punch - "this fighting is ridiculous. If we all agree to stop, we can share those sandwiches and be friends." The punches continue to fly from all sides, including from David, whilst each of them thinks about the proposition. None is prepared to stop punching whilst David's proposition is being considered. Then another boy, Pete, says: "Yeah, Dave is right. How about it?" The punches still continue to fly (though perhaps with a little less force). After a short while, however, the other two boys, also realising the futility of the fight, voice their agreement but it is only at that point of unanimous agreement that the punching actually stops. Until then, all the boys continued punching each other even though they were simultaneously negotiating about stopping.

In this example we can recognise a very basic human truth – that which separates man from animals: that humans are capable of operating on two levels. Even though we may be engaged in potentially mortal combat or some equally competitive activity against others, there is always the ability and possibility to simultaneously negotiate with them for peace. So we can maintain our competitive (punching) behaviour whilst at the same time proposing a cessation of competition and a commencement of co-operation subject to all others doing likewise. Furthermore, we can maintain that competitive behaviour for as long as it takes for all the competitors to agree to the proposition of co-operation. This is one of the paradoxes of the human condition: that we can, if needs must, do one thing whilst proposing the exact opposite. The recognition and understanding of this paradox is of profound importance to what follows in this paper. It may even prove to be our salvation.

We can also see other human truths in this example. We see the stages of community-building: firstly of violent and competitive Chaos; then of Emptiness brought about by communication, by letting bygones be bygones, and by accepting people for what they are. In emptying ourselves we come to see the futility of endless competition and violence to the point where we see the value of co-operation and Community – in short, we see the human truth of reconciliation.

THE NEED FOR LEADERSHIP

Important questions arise from the above example when considering how to ameliorate our two world problems of achieving Right Livelihood and Right Human Relations as well as ridding ourselves of the domination of global free markets. One key difference between boys fighting over sandwiches and nations competing in the international economy is one of self-control. In order to *co-operate* reliably with one another, each entity must first be able to '*operate*' reliably on its own: each must possess self-control and that ability must also be recognised and trusted by the others. The boys possess self-control in that each alone can decide on and control his actions and this is obvious to the others. National governments, conversely, do not posses the same measure of self-control but rely, to a large extent, on those who elect them to provide it.

So how can we, the electorate, provide national "self-control" in a way that brings governments to co-operate in implementing humanitarian, ecologically-aligned policies when we are operating in an electoral environment where politicians have only a highly restricted, short-term view and choosing one political party or another no longer makes any substantial difference?

Suddenly we begin to see the true depths of our impotence, finding ourselves bereft of the power of political choice we were led to believe democracy conferred upon us. We start to feel the extent to which the global economy has disempowered not only our politicians but, in consequence, also ourselves. But once we are no longer deluded by "democracy" and see it for the pseudo-democracy it really is, paradoxically we become liberated. Liberated in the sense that we no longer need to labour under the false illusion that voting for one or other party can offer any hope of the reforms our poor planet and so many of its people so urgently need. No longer need we remain fragmented and divided along party-political lines but, instead, we become free to rise above petty party politics: free to distance ourselves from that delusion and free to unite as citizens of the world, able to come together to look afresh and objectively at the global picture, however bad it may be. In our new-found freedom and objectivity, we firstly realise that we are subject to a quasi-dictatorship and that party politics offers no way out. We can therefore only look to ourselves. Secondly we realise that we have nothing to lose in attempting to develop an alternative and completely independent strategy. In the cold light of these liberating yet seemingly desperate circumstances, the questions we face in developing such a strategy are:

First, since most nations are wedded today to the idea of economic growth, global free markets and the capitalist system, why would they see the need for change to that system in any case?

Second, if they did see a need for change, how could they do so when nations fear, mistrust and compete with each other?

Third, if an appropriate strategy for answering the two preceding questions could be found, how could it be achieved in practice?

In addition to these questions, there remains the crucial and central problem of leadership. In our playground example, David appointed himself as leader by being first to propose a cessation of competition and the commencement of co-operation. In an international context, a similar initiative is needed. But who is to guide nations from competition to co-operation? Who will lead them through an era of Emptiness – the bridge between Chaos and Community? We have seen that it can be neither the UN nor our political leaders on their own. It can only come from a newly empowered and widespread political movement capable of providing it. In this crucial matter, there are two issues to be decided: One is to establish what measures will best solve or at least substantially ameliorate our two world problems. After all, if nations are to be guided towards agreement on a range of measures, we need to define what those measures should be.

Once that has been clarified, the other is the issue of promoting and achieving consensus between nations on implementing those measures. Some body or organisation is required, it seems, that can both facilitate a process for defining appropriate measures and have sufficient influence over nation states to bring them to consensus on implementing them.

Able to look only to ourselves to bring about meaningful and beneficial reform, the need for a new organisation both for facilitating the definition of the measures required to set us on the road to solving our two world problems and for building strong influence over nation states of all types is therefore essential. For non-democratic states, the aim of such an organisation must be to convince those in charge of the appropriateness of the proposed measures. For democratic states, on the other hand, its task is to organise and mobilise public opinion to force politicians to bring about their implementation. It is precisely for the performance of these crucial functions that the International Simultaneous

Policy Organisation (ISPO) has been established. But how can ISPO fulfil these highly ambitious functions and, moreover, how can it possibly succeed? Answers to all these questions and the associated issues above will be discussed in the following chapters.

5. Finding Solutions

"We jolly well have to have the courage to dream if we want to survive and give our children a chance of survival. The...crisis of which I have spoken will not go away if we simply carry on as before. It will become worse and end in disaster, until or unless we develop a new life-style which is compatible with the real needs of human nature, with the health of living nature around us, and with the resource endowment of the world."[1]

As the above quotation suggests, we must have the courage to dream − or at least to use our imaginations − if solutions to our current crisis are to be developed and pursued. Indeed, we must have the courage to think what may, perhaps at first glance, be considered unthinkable if we are ever to find a plausible way out of what is a dilemma of truly global proportions. So, if the reader will permit, a solution will be put forward in which many assumptions are made for I am neither an economist nor a political scientist. It is a solution which ISPO is currently developing with the help of growing numbers who have the vision to see the necessity of achieving the global simultaneous implementation of appropriate measures and who can also see this objective as perfectly feasible. Before discussing ISPO as an organisation, however, I will first set out an outline proposal for its policy.

[1] *Small is Beautiful*. E.F. Schumacher. Abacus, 1974.

THE SIMULTANEOUS POLICY

The aims, scope and principles of the Simultaneous Policy, as well as the measures it comprises, follow. The most important feature is that each of its measures is to be *implemented by all nations simultaneously.*

AIMS OF THE SIMULTANEOUS POLICY

The Simultaneous Policy has as its ultimate aim the transformation of the international economy such that it operates in harmony with the global natural environment and with the needs of human nature. This entails the transformation of those components of the capitalist system that can be described as global, large-scale or over-sized in such a way as to reduce their power and impact. Those components may be financial markets, corporations, institutions, technologies, etc. The Simultaneous Policy also has the aims of both an equitable consumption of natural resources amongst all people of the world and an overall level of consumption that is sustainable. It recognises that capitalism when practised on a relatively small human scale works very well and it does not therefore directly affect local, small or medium-scale enterprise. Its aim is not to destroy capitalism but rather to give it the legitimacy it currently lacks by ensuring the avoidance of the big and the promotion of the small. These aims could be summed up in the words: 'balance', 'peace' and 'permanence'.

The Simultaneous Policy's immediate aims are to restore genuine democracy by creating a genuine 'community of nation states' built upon consensus such that proper democratic control over global markets and corporations is restored. This will then permit the peoples of individual nations the freedom in which the Simultaneous Policy's overall aims can be independently pursued in a manner consistent with local conditions.

SCOPE OF THE SIMULTANEOUS POLICY

The scope of the Simultaneous Policy (hereafter "SP") is restricted to policies which, if implemented unilaterally by any nation or group of nations, would likely have adverse consequences for their competitiveness or for employment or capital markets. These are the policies which the world urgently requires but nations cannot implement because of the threat of capital flight or other undesirable effects. In addition to these could be added those policies which by their nature require a global approach.

Policies which have no adverse impact on national competitiveness, on the other hand, or which are of a more localised nature are clearly matters which concern only internal national affairs and consequently do not require simultaneous implementation. Such policies would therefore not fall within the scope of SP. SP could therefore be described as addressing itself purely to global issues and considered as complementary to regional, national or local initiatives rather than as an alternative to them. As such, SP can be said to synthesise the requirements of both global unity and national diversity.

MEASURES OF THE SIMULTANEOUS POLICY

Before proposing measures for SP, I should point out that these proposals and their implementation timetable are not made as a definitive statement of policy but more to demonstrate what *could* be possible. They are also made in the sense of 'throwing them into the cooking pot' along with those made by many leading ecologists, economists and others. Consensus on a final range of measures and an appropriate timetable would need to be arrived at which together would comprise the measures of SP. As such, it is the concept of *global simultaneous implementation* that is crucial for the purposes of this book rather than whatever the actual measures themselves turn out to be. In fact, provided they fall within the proper scope of SP, its measures can be *whatever those supporting SP decide them to be.* Let us assume, therefore, that appropriate measures can and will be formulated. Solely for the purpose of illustration, therefore, we shall proceed on the basis of the proposed measures that follow.

Three stages of measures are proposed here which would be implemented in all countries simultaneously over, say, a 10 -15 year period:

1st Stage-Year 1: Implementation of stabilisation measures of current global financial markets by re-regulating them, thus reversing the de-regulation that has been the case hitherto. The main idea here is to bring stability to our current global financial system to make it 'safe' for further reforms to be carried out.

A further measure would be removal of the issuing of credit from the commercial banks and its restoration to state control. (Monetary Reform).

Another necessary measure would be the dismantling and banning of all nuclear weapons.

A further important stabilisation measure would be the banning of political funding by business (or at least by big business) in order to restore proper independence and public accountability to politics.

Third World Debt would be cancelled but only under certain conditions which will be discussed later.

Stabilisation is also required in the fields of science and technology. Measures would be needed if not to halt research into genetic engineering of living beings and plants then to ban its general application in agriculture, industry, medicine and elsewhere.

2nd Stage-Year 3: Implementation of access measures to provide the necessary access to the boardrooms of major institutions and corporations. The decisions that cause our problems are formulated and executed in the boardrooms of major corporations and institutions. The reform we see as being necessary should therefore be brought about, I suggest, by gaining direct access to them.

3rd Stage-Years 5 - 15: The implementation of a wide variety of change measures to transform major corporations and institutions into ones that are more compatible with a healthy society and environment. Such a wide variety of measures will need to be implemented, step by step, in 'sub-stages', each of which is to be implemented in all countries simultaneously.

Let us look briefly at what is intended for each of these three stages.

STABILISATION MEASURES (1ST STAGE-YEAR 1)

In the first instance, we need to put a stop to the worst aspects of global currency speculation, i.e. the 'casino economy' and generally to limit the free movement of capital to a point where a reasonable level of stability can be counted upon. Such measures would doubtless include regulations concerning corporate 'transfer pricing' and the Tobin Tax. (George Soros puts forward a series of proposals that might well meet this requirement in *The Crisis of Global Capitalism*, chapter 8).

(I would add that, at the rate financial markets are going, the stabilisation measures proposed are likely to have already been implemented as a result of a major crisis long before the Simultaneous Policy is implemented. If adequate measures are taken as a result, they can be deleted from this proposal.)

The need to remove the issuing of credit from the commercial banks and to restore it to state control (Monetary Reform) also represents an essential measure to stabilise and democratise both global and national economies. About 97% of all money in circulation has been issued as debt by the commercial banks upon which interest must be paid yet this debt is not substantially backed by deposits. The need to service ever-larger debts and interest payments forces borrowers - be they individuals, businesses or governments – to compete ever more fiercely to earn sufficient money to repay both loan and interest. This is a key factor which drives both rich and poor nations to seek debt-free revenues through higher exports in order to meet interest payments on previous debts. Such a financial system which contains the seeds of its own (and everyone else's) destruction must therefore be reformed.[2]

In spite of the end of the Cold War, nuclear and other weapons of mass destruction still remain a considerable threat to world peace. Their justification is usually argued on the basis of deterrence: a form of competition based on threat. However, General Lee Butler, former Commander-in-Chief of US Strategic Command, now points out that:

> "Deterrence failed completely as a guide in setting rational limits on the size and composition of military forces. To the contrary, its appetite was voracious, its capacity to justify new weapons and larger stocks unrestrained. Deterrence carried the

---

[2] Interesting proposals for monetary reform are made by Alan D. Armstrong in *To Restrain the Red Horse*. Towerhouse Publishing, 1996 and by Frances Hutchinson in *What Everybody Really Wants to know about Money*, Jon Carpenter Publishing, 1998. I should point out that proponents of monetary reform generally insist that it could be implemented by any nation unilaterally without any adverse impact on competitiveness, capital markets, etc. Surely, however, the banks would seek to veto such a reform by threatening to move jobs abroad. Indeed, such a basic policy shift would be unlikely to be implemented unilaterally by any government, I suggest, simply because they are unsure and distrustful of the effects of those reforms and fear, perhaps wrongly, for national competitiveness. It may be, therefore, that global simultaneous implementation may provide the only circumstances under which governments would be prepared to take the risk, knowing that all other nations would be in the same boat. (More fundamental proposals for reforms to the capitalist system are explained by the late Folkert Wilken in *The Liberation of Capital*.)

seed, born of an irresolvable internal contradiction, that spurred an insatiable arms race."[3]

A cessation of the wholly inappropriate and damaging intrusion of corporate funding into politics is another stabilising action required to put an end to the distortion of democratic processes. Actions to limit or eliminate corporate manipulation through 'front organisations', think-tanks and the media would also be necessary.[4] Instead, funding of political parties should come from public funds on an equitable basis.

The oppressive burden of debt on poorer countries must finally be put to an end. But simply cancelling it fails to provide a satisfactory answer because, under the current system, the basis upon which any future funds are provided would still require the payment of interest which only serves to increase dependency. Furthermore, most investment in such countries fails to reach the people who most need it, benefiting instead a restricted elite mainly based in their cities. If their debts are to be cancelled, these countries should be required to ensure that development programmes are geared to long-term economic self-reliance and designed to benefit directly the widest possible number of the neediest people.

Similarly, until the full effects of the impact of genetic engineering can be properly and ethically assessed, we need to stabilise the situation by preventing its application on a global basis and by phasing out such use that exists already. Other similar measures in other fields may also be required.

A further and necessary stabilisation measure would be to adjust the laws of each country to effect the abolition of all tax havens that today provide the rich and the criminal fraternities with means of avoiding their tax obligations.

[3] Quoted from *Resurgence* No. 193. March/April 1999.
[4] The need for this is well documented in *Global Spin*. Sharon Beder. Green Books, 1997.

ACCESS MEASURES (2ND STAGE-YEAR 3)

As far as access measures are concerned, the proposal here is to reform the system from the inside rather than trying in vain to do it only by regulation and pricing mechanisms, as it were, from the outside. After all, changing a system from within is usually quicker and far more effective. This idea was originally expounded by Schumacher in "Small is Beautiful".[5] Whilst I believe his principles remain valid, parts of his proposal require updating and refining. For the moment, however, the first step could broadly be as follows:

> Abolish corporation tax and substitute it with the government holding a percentage (say 30%) of shares in all major companies. Corporation Tax revenue would thus be substituted by dividends. This would avoid the "us and them" mentality that pervades the relationship between Business and Government and all that goes with it as explained in detail by Schumacher;

> More importantly, by dint of its shareholding, the government would be entitled to appoint a similar or possibly greater percentage of "special directors" to the board. This would be done in such a way that a veto could, if necessary and after due process, be exercised by them on actions likely to affect not only the company's local environment but also it's global operations. Similarly, "special directors" would also be appointed to major financial and other institutions with the same powers. As such, restraint could be brought to bear directly at the heart of corporate and institutional decision-making.

The increasing power of TNCs and their ability to influence government policy, often by threatening to move production to some other country, has given rise to growing calls for greater regulation to afford a greater measure of control over them. Regulation has, however, proved to be only partially effective particularly in developing countries where the

---

[5] *Small is Beautiful.* Abacus, 1974. Pages 239–245.

capacity for enforcement is severely limited. It is also clear that TNCs and other major corporations are expert at circumventing regulations and, as has been pointed out, few governments are willing to regulate them whilst they threaten to move investment – and therefore jobs - elsewhere. In contrast to regulation, therefore, the direct access of 'special directors' to board and management information would thus allow them, after due process, to ensure that potentially harmful activities could be restrained before they occur. Furthermore, the 'special directors' would have a far more direct, dynamic and meaningful influence on many other issues, ranging from environmental restraint to social issues and from ownership to development issues. In the case of arms manufacturers, for example, 'special directors' by their power of veto, could ensure that all sales were strictly consistent with an appropriate global code of conduct. 'Special directors' would *not*, however, be responsible either to their corporations or to governments. This will be explained more fully in chapter 8. For the sake of brevity, this proposal is referred to as the 'Corporation Tax for Equity Swap' in later chapters.

CHANGE MEASURES (3RD STAGE-YEARS 5 - 15)

Having considered the 'stabilisation' and 'access' measures which allow actual reform to be safely and effectively applied to the capitalist system, it is the 'change measures' themselves that clearly present the biggest challenge. The reader will recall that these would be implemented over a ten year period and would be broken down into sub-stages. Very many far-reaching measures will undoubtedly be required.

One such measure should, I propose, be a tax on corporate profits. This tax, referred to in later chapters as the 'Development Tax' would be used exclusively to fund development in the world's poorest and least developed countries on a debt-free basis. It would represent a kind of Marshall Plan for non-industrialised and less developed countries. As mentioned above, in exchange for cancelling their debt mountain, these nations would have to commit themselves as a matter of national policy to development programmes which can be demonstrated to directly benefit the poorest and to foster economic growth geared to their future self-reliance rather than growth geared to dependency. The 'Development Tax' would strongly augment the already sub-stantial sums to be raised by implementation of the Tobin Tax.

In this way, both a long term funnel of funds from North to South could be assured as well as the knowledge that such funds would be spent wisely. After all, if all major corporations worldwide are subject to this tax, not only will issues of com-petition not arise but the whole programme of development for poorer countries could be boosted in a way hitherto unimaginable. Whilst current campaigning to reduce or cancel 'third world debt' is welcome and necessary, it is not enough. Unless far-reaching reform to the financial system is implemented, even the cancellation of 'third world debt' tomorrow would only mean it would very soon reappear. Poor countries therefore need to commit themselves to self-reliant development bolstered by freely donated funds from the North, which in the long run remains the only means of ensuring sustainable development, the widest possible pros-perity of their peoples, and a consequent slowing of rampant population growth, disease, warfare and refugees. The Development and Tobin taxes would be the cornerstones of a reorientation of the international economy towards regional, national and local self-reliance similar to that proposed by Lang and Hines and by Ted Dunn.[6]

---

[6] *The New Protectionism.* Tim Lang and Colin Hines. Earthscan 1993. *Regional Peace and Development Programmes.* Ted Dunn, The Alternatives to War Press, 1993. Also, *Localization - A Global Manifesto.* Colin Hines. Earthscan, 2000.

Further reforms could also be included along with a complete reappraisal of capitalism's incorrect assumption that God-given natural resources, land and intellectual property should accrue solely to the benefit of their owners. Any such reforms would, however, not necessarily mean taking them into the control of the state but instead that their owners could, in some instances, become trustees of those assets on behalf of society as whole.

Deciding on change measures represents a challenge not only in terms of what reforms should occur and in what order, but in particular, what reforms the public around the world could identify as being ones that it would find willing to wholeheartedly support. Would the admittedly far-reaching 'stabilisation' and 'access' measures already proposed in themselves be sufficient to gain strong and widespread public support for SP? It is a difficult question to answer but will be dealt with in more detail in later chapters.

Of course global simultaneous implementation appears – and indeed is – highly ambitious to say the least. However, we shall nevertheless proceed to answer the three questions put at the end of the previous chapter and demonstrate that, if the people desire it, it can be achieved. Before doing so, however, the other principles of the Simultaneous Policy must also be properly understood for they are, together, just as important as simultaneous implementation itself.

PRINCIPLES OF THE SIMULTANEOUS POLICY

The Simultaneous Policy is capable of gaining widespread support amongst individuals of whatever race, colour, creed or nationality; amongst organisations of any type: businesses, non-government organisations, schools, hospitals, sports clubs, religious groups, etc.; amongst political parties of almost any leaning and amongst governments of any type: democratic, single party, monarchy, dictatorship, etc.

Its ethos is therefore one of accepting people, organisations and nations for what they are, without judgement, in the interests of the sustained future of the planet and in the interest of the common future and well-being of humanity. This does not imply that change is not required; on the contrary. It is merely a recognition that no state, organisation or person is perfect and, proceeding from this, that all should strive, in their own way, towards achieving open and democratic societies.

The principles governing its adoption and implementation are:

1. The distinction between adoption and implementation.

Since *implementation* is to be simultaneous amongst all nations, it can only occur once *adoption* by all nations has been achieved. It is therefore clear that a gradual process of adoption or 'adoption campaign' must take place first: person by person, party by party, nation by nation.

2. Universal Inclusiveness: SP may be adopted by anyone.

Any individual, any organisation, any political party or any government may adopt SP provided it (i.e. all the measures it comprises) is adopted in full. As has been pointed out, ISPO has been created to organise and encourage this process.

For individuals, businesses or other non-governmental organisations, adoption of SP simply signifies their open support for it, their desire for the political party or government of their choice to adopt it, and their own open 'declaration of intent' to support and abide by its measures when they are eventually implemented. In effect, having adopted SP, each would be saying to the rest of the world: "Hey! I've adopted. I'm ready to implement as soon as you all are. How about it?" Until adoption by all nation states is actually achieved, such individuals, parties or organisations need not alter their current views or behaviour in any way.

3. Adoption by political parties or governments: special conditions.

For political parties or governments of any kind, adoption is on the strict understanding that its measures are accepted in full and that they will start to implement them in a coordinated fashion as soon as universal adoption has been achieved. (It may be that ISPO might need to underpin this by entering into a contract of some kind, presumably governed by international law.) Implementation of a uniform set of measures would thus occur simultaneously on a global basis. Adoption of SP could therefore be described as an open 'declaration of intent' to implement its measures when all others do likewise. It should be clear to the reader that this mirrors our playground lesson of fighting over sandwiches. They would be officially identifying themselves to their public, to their political competitors and to all other governments around the world, effectively saying:

> "We continue to implement all our current policies exactly as before and to maintain our country's competitive position in world markets. Whilst doing so, however, we have additionally adopted SP which we will only implement when all other nations do likewise. In adopting it, we call upon all political parties and governments of the world to follow our example."

Adoption of SP therefore means that any political party or government can continue to pursue their current policies exactly as before. It is only when the governments of *all* nations have adopted that competition ceases and co-operation begins.

Unlike many other initiatives, charters and declarations calling for global reform, SP is different in the crucial respect that it separates 'adoption' from 'implementation' *and* provides a secure basis upon which implementation can occur. This renders it capable of official adoption by political parties and governments. It therefore possesses the political and practical framework other initiatives lack and explains why, even when widely supported, those initiatives are rarely, if ever, put into practice.

4. The distinction between current and future policy contexts.

Since global simultaneous implementation refers to a point in time in the future at which all governments implement the same measures, this could be described as a 'future context' of co-operation amongst nations - the new era of international global Community. This is quite distinct and different from the period of time prior to that point which (even though the gradual process of adoption may be occurring) can be described as the 'current context', as we have it today, which is one of competition amongst nations - the continued era of competitive chaos.

The contexts of co-operation (future) and competition (current) are clearly entirely different if not opposite in nature. After all, competition is the opposite of cooperation. But like fighting over sandwiches there is a paradox: a measure that might be completely unthinkable in the current competitive context can also be entirely practical and desirable in the future co-operative context. For example, in a context of competition, it would be unthinkable for one or a group of nations to re-regulate their financial markets whilst all others were left unregulated. For the country or group of countries doing so it would be financially highly disadvantageous, if not suicidal. Re-regulation of financial markets on that basis therefore remains a proposition with only theoretical appeal and because it is impractical, it remains sterile. If, on the other hand, all nations did so together, i.e. in a context of co-operation, the self-same proposition would not only be thinkable and practical – it also becomes desirable. What was a sterile proposition thus becomes extremely fertile. This is the power of co-operation and Community. That what has just been explained is rather obvious only tends to underscore the extent to which this power seems today to have been forgotten by so many. In effect therefore, individuals, political parties and others will have two parallel sets of views or policies: one set for the 'current context' which is in an active state and comprises their current views, policies and behaviour as set out in their current manifesto, and one set for the as yet inactive 'future context' which would comprise, (when they have chosen to adopt it), the measures of SP.

5. The Principles of Openness and Challenge

In recognising that we can still engage in a policy of punching (i.e. competing with) one another whilst we may, at the same time, be advocating co-operation in the form of adoption of SP, we see that, like the boys fighting over sandwiches, we can carry on with these two policies of 'punching' and 'advocating' in parallel for as long as is necessary until all parties agree. Similarly, nations can continue to slug it out with one another in a competitive context whilst some may at the same time have adopted (but not implemented) SP, signifying their commitment and desire to co-operate with one another as soon as all others do the same.

However, in doing so, those that have adopted SP also need to openly advertise that fact to those who have not yet done so: they need to openly communicate the fact. This applies to individuals, organisations, businesses, political parties and governments alike. In doing so, they set a challenge to others to adopt it and inherent in this challenge is a simple question: Why haven't you adopted it yet? As the numbers choosing to adopt gradually increase, so the moral force of the challenge will similarly increase. Again, a seemingly obvious point. However, in the context of our two world problems that daily become ever clearer to us, such openness and challenge are surely just what the world needs.

Another aspect of the adoption campaign would be its openness in confronting problems that have hitherto remained largely under the carpet and consequently outside mainstream political debate. In seeing those who openly advertise their adoption of SP, it encourages those who have not yet adopted to be similarly open in discussing our two world problems as well as many other related issues. Knowing that implementation can only occur once all nations agree, allows people the freedom to do so. Once they see that others are not embarrassed to admit these problems, so they will feel more able to openly discuss them together. Public and open debate should therefore ensue leading to a more vibrant discussion all round. If sharing a problem with others is a major part of the road to its solution, then this can only be a good thing.

6. The principle of the Simultaneous Policy as being non-party political.

This arises as a consequence of the distinction between current and future contexts. The boys fighting over the sandwiches may have ended up in the fight for all sorts of reasons. They may be from different backgrounds or hold different views. When it comes to advocating a sharing of the sandwiches, those reasons and differences are put to one side in the common interest of reaching the future context of co-operation: eating the sand-wiches. None of the boys at that point particularly cares what each others reasons may have been for entering the fight or what their differences may have been or who started it. In agreeing to share the sandwiches, each puts his own and the other's current competitive behaviour (or politics) to one side.

Similarly, whatever the current politics of a person, organisation or political party, if they consider the measures of SP as desirable in a future context in which all co-operate, that is all that matters. Any differences in their current politics or behaviour become irrelevant and therefore have no signif-icant impact, if any, on what they agree to do together in future: implement SP. In this way, it renders SP capable of being adopted by almost any person, any organisation or by almost any political party. Because it relates only to the future co-operative context, SP becomes a non-party political issue in the current competitive context. As will be seen, this has profound and far-reaching implications but is, in fact, nothing more than another simple human truth. The truth of recon-ciliation in which we 'let bygones be bygones'.

In letting bygones be bygones we also recognise that no one can really be blamed for our capitalist system and its shortcomings: or perhaps more accurately, we are *all* to blame. Even the world's business leaders are as helpless to change things as anyone else, locked as they are into a mode of preda-tory competition from which there is ordinarily no way out.

7. The Principle of National Sovereignty

Since SP in any case depends on the consensus of all nation states, no fundamental question of usurping of state power arises.

Once the adoption by all national governments has been achieved, the 'current competitive context' of policy is at an end and the 'future co-operative context' begins immediately with the implementation of SP measures. Further measures beyond those proposed could be added at a later date always provided they are adopted and implemented in the same fashion. The process is therefore capable of continuation provided any additional measures fall within the proper scope of SP.

FROM THEORY TO PRACTICE

The concept of simultaneous implementation on a global basis is vital because it eliminates any possible difference of policy between nations. It also eliminates any possible difference in the time of implementation. Therefore, any institution or corporation, transnational or otherwise, can and need take no steps to attempt to circumvent the eventual effects of implementation by relocating their domicile because there would be no other country available that would offer them any advantage of any kind.

Let us, however, remind ourselves that we are seeking to directly treat the root cause of our world problems. In seeking solutions, our first question was:

> Since most nations are as wedded today to the idea of economic growth, global free markets and the capitalist system, why would they see the need for change to that system in any case?

If we assume the worst case scenario and suppose that they do not see any such need, we must firstly make clear to politicians what is being asked of them. Politicians, being preoccupied with slugging it out in the current context of competition and being prey to influence by big business cannot be expected to see that free market fundamentalism is plainly damaging; nor that their espousal of economic growth is but a hollow response to environmental and other world problems. Neither can they be expected to see a method for finding a way out. This, as I have pointed out, is why the International Simultaneous Policy Organisation (ISPO) has been established both to facilitate a process for defining the measures of SP and to bring nation states to adopt it. However, we are still faced with the question not only of convincing governments of the need to adopt it but also the practical problem of how to bring them to actually do so. Before returning to answer them, however, we can at least already answer our second question which was:

> If politicians did see a need for change, how could they do so when nations fear, mistrust and compete with one another?

As should be clear from the principles of SP listed above, global simultaneous implementation itself eliminates mistrust and competition because it puts all nations in exactly the same boat. The condition of simultaneous implementation permits them to see the measures of SP in the context of nations co-operating with one another in their implementation – i.e. to see it in a *future context* that is quite separate from the current one. In terms of that future context, therefore, fear, mistrust and competition at the international level simply evaporate.

The method of global simultaneous implementation could be regarded as a logical extension to methods now being used in the EU to implement new policy, be it the single currency or other measures. As far as possible these are being implemented simultaneously across Europe to avoid variations or loopholes – i.e. competition - between member states; variations that would be used by corporations or others to gain competitive advantages which could have an adverse effect on employment in some member states. A further example might be the recent calls for a policy of "tax harmonisation" amongst EU member states. (It should, however, be understood that I do not necessarily support the single European currency or some other measures being implemented in the EU – in fact I don't. What I am pointing out is solely *the method* that simultaneous implementation represents.) A few years ago, implementation in this style would have seemed ludicrous. With global communications and economies as integrated as they are today, however, I see no reason why global simultaneous implementation of a set of measures need any longer be considered as out of the question. Indeed, it is surely vital.

Failure to do so would carry the very real risk that transnational corporations or financial markets would simply move their domicile to some other country to avoid implementation, involving capital flight, a loss of jobs, etc. In such circumstances, corporations would indeed be quite right to do so as their competitors domiciled in countries not implementing SP could be said to have an unfair competitive advantage. However, if all countries implemented it simultaneously, what valid objection could big business and institutions (or indeed any of us) have?

Persuading all countries to adopt SP sounds like an incredibly tall order, and indeed it is. As we have seen however, such is the enormity of the problem that anything less will *simply fail* because, like individual companies, no country or group of countries or their government(s) would ever be naïve enough to risk their economic competitiveness, jobs and therefore votes unless all others were in the same boat. A global problem therefore requires a global - and simultaneous – solution. Ambitious this may indeed be, but let us think about it for a moment. Surely, global simultaneous implementation actually represents a low-risk way forward in that it removes the key fear of business, governments and people alike: the possibility that *some* major corporations or *some* countries could gain unfair competitive advantage by escaping implementation thus causing a loss of competitiveness, profitability, jobs and votes for all others. In short, by eliminating competition at this level, we also eliminate its adverse consequences. At the same time, we also eliminate fear and mistrust. This is the essence of SP.

Whilst the concept of global simultaneous implementation appears, and doubtless remains, a highly challenging target, it nevertheless represents the only *appropriate basis* upon which the leaders of nation states, businesses, institutions and, in fact, all members of society around the world, can safely contemplate and discuss practical and beneficial reform. Without that basis, the world can only remain locked into the vicious circle of competition, leaving its leaders unable even to talk meaningfully of co-operation because, neither knowing what measures might be appropriate to solve world problems nor having an appropriate basis upon which co-operation could occur, any proposals for reform would either be unworkable and lead to endless frustration or be seen as a sign of weakness in a competitive context where the ethic of pursuing the 'national interest' inevitably reigns supreme. Under such circumstances, talk of co-operation effectively remains impossible. Identifying global simultaneous implementation as the appropriate basis for safe and secure communication therefore allows us to break our enforced silence and to start *communicating* meaningfully with one another about co-operation without risking our positions in the current context of competition. For without meaningful communication, disaster inevitably becomes a certainty. However ambitious and unlikely its achievement may be, therefore, providing and articulating global simultaneous implementation as the appropriate basis for co-operation actually represents our key to salvation.

To sum up, *simultaneity* with respect to SP applies in two ways: firstly that two seemingly opposing policies are pursued simultaneously in parallel; one policy comprising current competitive behaviour, the other a declaration of intent for future co-operative behaviour. Secondly, that implementation eventually takes place in all countries simultaneously. Without the concept of a distinct and separate future context of co-operative behaviour between nations, world political leaders remain locked within the competitive constraints of current conventional politics, able at best to make only marginal adjustments to social and economic policies. Without global simultaneous implementation, global free financial markets can only continue to exert their strangle-hold over the national domestic policy agenda of any nation. Neither the unravelling of social cohesion in advanced countries nor the two world problems of the global environment and the poor can ever be substantially improved within a framework of action that permits only marginal and incremental measures, rather than an overhaul of policy and a questioning of underlying values. This is precisely why targets for reducing global warming emissions or other such targets are hardly worth the paper they are printed on. They remain merely words without action because the action required to achieve them itself requires fundamental reforms to the capitalist system: reforms which against the background of competing nations and global free capital markets can only be effectively brought about through global simultaneous implementation.

A gradual process of adoption of SP prior to implementation allows nations to adopt it whilst at the same time maintaining their current competitive behaviour. It signifies to all others their commitment to implement it when all are prepared to do likewise. It similarly allows politicians to adopt it without risking their personal positions in the secure knowledge that implementation can only occur when all other nations do likewise. This is the only way to eliminate competition, mistrust and fear at the international level as well as their damaging effects which permeate all levels of society. Everyone, from top to bottom, knows that in adopting SP they in no way risk their current positions and, similarly, if and when implementation occurs, everyone is subject to precisely the same effects.[7]

The adoption process could be likened to a bridge that spans the stages of Chaos and Community. In terms of world Community-building, the adoption process could *itself* be described as the stage of Emptiness. As each person, organisation or political party adopts SP, they recognise the futility and damage done by continued unfettered competition; they recognise the flaws of our capitalist system and are prepared to be seen both to admit them and stand ready to address them. In adopting SP they join what is gradually becoming a growing throng of people throughout the world that yearns for the restoration of genuine democracy, for international co-operation, peace and community. To reach Community, we must pass through the stage of Emptiness. In adopting SP therefore, even though their behaviour and other views remain essentially as before, they crucially identify themselves to those around them as ready to implement SP and, by the same token, challenge them to do likewise. In adopting SP, one could say that they join the *"march through emptiness"*.

Assuming that the content of SP has been defined and knowing that global simultaneous implementation answers

---

[7] It should be clear that SP seeks only to eliminate competition at the nation state level as a means of regaining democratic control over capital markets and major corporations. Whilst major issues of taxation and regulation of major corporations and institutions would be covered by SP, *healthy* competition between corporations and at other levels in society would remain untouched. The overall result should therefore be a *framework* of co-operation within which healthy competition can flourish.

our second question concerning competition and mistrust between nation states, let us now return to our first question which was:

> Since most nations are wedded today to the idea of economic growth, global free markets and the capitalist system, why would they see the need for change to that system in any case?

In the developed world consisting largely of the advanced democratic nations of the north, convincing them of that need can only occur through the ballot box. As will be seen, however, pseudo-democracy requires that SP's use of the ballot box must necessarily be unconventional. Were we still to be labouring under the delusion that party politics could offer us the reforms so sorely needed, one might assume that ISPO might be a new political party with branches in each country. However, it is clear that under pseudo-democracy, the obsolescence of political parties both demands and allows us to take a more elegant approach. ISPO has therefore been established as:

an international campaigning and lobbying organisation that has as its main objective the persuasion of one or more mainstream political parties in each country to adopt SP.

Difficult though the achievement of this objective may appear, let us continue to apply our imagination and take a closer look. Before explaining in greater detail the activities and structure of ISPO, in the following two chapters we will first discuss the feasibility of its objective.

6. SP: Adoption by Advanced Democratic Countries

"Unity and right human relations - individual, communal, national and international - can be brought about by the united action of the men and women of goodwill in every country. These men and women of goodwill must be found and organized and thus discover their numerical potency - for it is there. They must form a world group, standing for right human relations and educating the public in the nature and power of goodwill. They will thus create a world public opinion which will be so forceful and so outspoken on the side of human welfare that leaders, statesmen, politicians, businessmen and churchmen will be forced to listen and comply."[1]

Alice Bailey

As has been implied, the key to universal adoption of SP will be to secure adoption by the developed nations, these consisting largely of the advanced (pseudo-)democratic countries. Whilst it may be true to say that they cannot control global markets without the co-operation of most, if not all, other countries, their dominant influence over, and share of, the world's economic and military power is indisputable. Much of the active effort required in the adoption process will therefore take place in these countries. For non-industrialised and developing nations, on the other hand, whilst the main object of adoption would primarily be to signify the

---

[1] *Problems of Humanity.* Alice A. Bailey. Lucis Publishing Co, 1947. (Italic emphasis is hers.)

denial of their territories to any institution or corporation seeking to circumvent the regulation that SP would bring, it is the advanced democracies of the North that will require the most attention.

Many in advanced countries lament the stagnation of politics and call for democratic renewal characterised by truly free and open societies. However, such objectives can only be achieved if the people themselves are ready to act. Today we easily forget that universal suffrage was a hard-won right. With global markets now degrading democracy worldwide through the subtle imposition of pseudo-democracy, one would logically consider any attempt to achieve reform of the system through the ballot box as futile. Paradoxically, however, the ballot box still remains the only safety valve through which essential reforms can come about, without the danger of revolutionary or violent change. But this can only occur if we learn to use democratic processes in a completely new and unorthodox way; a way that transcends party politics and brings political parties into competition with one another to adopt SP.

We must firstly remember that pseudo-democracy means – perhaps for the first time in the history of democracy – that it now makes little, if any, difference which party we vote for. This is also, doubtless, an important reason explaining the ever-lower voter turn-outs in elections around the world. Whilst the effective obsolescence of political parties might appear to confirm our complete impotence, paradoxically it actually presents us with a unique opportunity. For we are now no longer duped by political parties knowing that, once elected, all of them must necessarily submit to market and corporate demands and we can instead concentrate solely on the objective of persuading *any* or even *more than one* mainstream party to adopt SP. For if sufficient voters can unite behind an alternative political agenda such as SP, they potentially represent a powerful force for beneficial reform.

Once existing political parties realise that a significant proportion of the electorate has both united behind an alternative agenda and is prepared to vote for *any* party that adopts it, the parties inevitably come into stiff competition with one another to be first to adopt it in order to attract the support of all those voters: the vital additional support that could make the difference between winning or losing an election. In this and the following chapter, we shall discuss the feasibility of this novel approach in achieving our objective.

In seeking the adoption of SP by one or more main-stream political parties, the lobbying organisation's first objective would be to devise the best individual strategy for each country most likely to result in adoption by at least one of the largest parties. It is of no concern to the lobbying group which party adopts SP or what their other day to day policies might be, for as we have seen, not only is there little differ-ence between the current policies of mainstream parties, those policies in any case have no relevance to us because SP applies solely to the future context of co-operation; a context which comes into existence only once global adoption has been achieved. However, as we shall see, the method of achieving their adoption is indirect. In what follows, the case for adoption by mainstream political parties will be argued mainly in the context of UK politics. As many know, with its two-party 'first past the post' electoral system, it is not a very democratic country and should therefore serve as a reason-ably fair example.

SP: IDEOLOGICAL CONFLICTS

Whilst it relates only to the future context of co-operation amongst nations it is important to recognise that SP is never-theless economically interventionist by nature. That is to say, its measures seek to intervene into economic affairs. This is diametrically opposed to the currently pervading free-market ideology which propounds the complete reign of the market. As such, political parties wedded to free-market ideology would be unlikely to adopt SP because, whether or not it relates only to the future context of co-operation, the resulting ideological conflict would be inherently untenable. As such, we should assume for the time being that centre-right (the Conservative party) and far-right parties are ruled out.

Many of the world's centre-left parties could, at first glance, also be said to fall into this category. To the extent that, today, they too embrace or at least reluctantly accept free-market ideology, one could argue that inherent conflict with SP might arise with them also. I suggest, however, that centre-left adoption of free market ideology is only skin-deep. The dictates of global free financial markets have narrowed the workable parameters of national economic and social policies such that, in order to gain power, centre-left parties had no option but to accept free market ideology and its consequences if they were ever to be elected. Instead of freely choosing their own position, therefore, all political parties are now competing with one another to position themselves most appropriately to what the market dictates. (Parties that fail to do so, like the Green parties, condemn themselves to eternal marginalisation.) In spite of the political demands of the market, however, the traditions of centre-left parties are, by and large, impeccably interventionist by nature and social-democratic in outlook. Their adoption of SP could therefore be justified on the principle of its relevance only to the future context of co-operation. In this way, leaders of centre-left parties seeking to adopt SP could argue that,

> "In the current context of competition, we need to be as competitive as the next country, and whilst that situation persists, we will continue to embrace free market economics in the same vein and 'give as good as we get' in the international competitive

environment. On the other hand, a future context of co-operation would allow us to return to our true heritage and belief in economic intervention and social democratic principles. If and when all other countries do likewise, global co-operation between us and all other states in the form of SP will allow us to return to our true roots and ensure that both the demands of competition and co-operation, and those of the market and a healthy society, are brought properly into balance."

So adoption of SP could, I suggest, be quite plausibly justified. Indeed, this demonstrates aptly how politicians could justify the adoption of SP without risking their current position nor that of their party or country. After all, no one could accuse them of deserting the national or party interest since they would be maintaining it in the current competitive context whilst simultaneously promoting it in a future co-operative context. The recent acceptance by centre-left parties of free market ideology need not therefore be a barrier to their adoption of SP in principle; in fact rather the contrary. Their adoption would permit them to reconcile their traditional social-democratic values that require economic intervention with the current realities of global free-market competition. The question that remains, therefore, is how to bring them to the point where they wish to adopt SP, for there are other barriers that must be overcome.

SP: OVERCOMING POLITICAL FUNDING FROM BIG BUSINESS

A further barrier to their adoption is their significant and growing dependence upon big business for funding. Clearly, adoption of SP by a centre-left party would be seen by their corporate supporters as a major assault on their freedom of action. It would therefore likely alienate those sources of funding thus rendering adoption by centre-left parties thinkable in ideological terms but impractical in financial terms.

Let us therefore leave centre-left parties be for the moment. Because there are "third" parties in most western democracies, (such as the Liberal Democrats in the UK), who are neither in the pockets of big business, nor can they be said to be outside the political mainstream. I will therefore confine my discussion only to "third" parties for the moment, for the problem of corporate funding in politics is, by its very nature, not one that can be tackled head-on. As will be argued during the remainder of this chapter, however, it can nevertheless be effectively dealt with.

SP: 'THIRD' PARTY ADOPTION

The proposition is that we would simply be asking a "third" party – the Liberal Democrats – to adopt SP, as has been described above, as a 'declaration of intent' relating to the future context of co-operation. As previously explained, this does not mean ditching or changing their current policies. These relate to the current context and therefore remain intact.

The first question that arises is whether SP would conflict ideologically with any of a third party's policies or ethos in terms of the measures proposed in chapter 5. Whilst the placing of "special directors" on the boards of all major corporations and other institutions and the other measures proposed (or some other similar range of measures) are far-reaching policies in themselves, I suggest that there would be no actual conflict either in terms of ideology or ethos.

The second question is whether adoption would make a mainstream "third" party appear too risky to vote for. In adopting SP, again we need to remember that implementation can only occur once adoption by all nations has been achieved. As such, adoption of SP has no effect on the current policies of a political party until global adoption occurs. Like fighting in the playground over sandwiches, a third party would fully maintain all of its current policies but, in adopting SP, would additionally be advocating fundamental reform of the world economy - reform which would only occur once all other nations agreed. Adoption therefore represents absolutely no risk. On the contrary, it would differentiate that party in a crucial way from its political competitors. It would be seen as the only party with two parallel sets of policies: one, as laid out in their current manifesto, which is designed for the current context of competition; the other, designed for a future context of global co-operation which takes the form of SP. Far from being seen as risky, it would surely be seen as the only party offering a genuine and practical way forward which, while world-wide agreement is being sought, takes no chances with our current system. This is important because it would demonstrate that there would be nothing to lose by *adoption* in the current competitive context because *implementation* could only occur in a future context of global co-operation.

In fact, because all main parties today have broadly similar policies designed as they are only for the current competitive context, there is consequently little to see between them. Indeed, the fact that differences between main parties are becoming blurred and insignificant makes today's politics appear meaningless and, frankly, so desperately boring! Moreover, the effective veto over public policy exercised by world markets makes this convergence of policy entirely inevitable. If a 'third' party adopted SP, therefore, that really *would* be different. It would be the only party advocating a world policy for the future that challenges others to do likewise. It would therefore become the focus of discussion and media attention. Indeed, the whole adoption process would inject new life into politics in every (pseudo-)democratic country in a way that little else could. This in itself is an important point not to be under-estimated because it would focus media and public debate on SP.

The current lack of any perceptible difference between mainstream parties is equally important when considering the third question of whether a mainstream "third" party could identify adoption of SP as an electoral advantage. The result of this lack of difference between the policies of today's political parties is that it is becoming far easier and less unusual for mainstream party voters to swap their allegiance from one mainstream party to another. After all, seeing little if any difference between them, what difference does voting for one or other make? With this in mind, the growth in the membership of environmental and other pressure groups[2] tells us that there are large and growing numbers in western (pseudo-) democracies who feel moved to do something for the environment and the poor but who passively continue to support any of the mainstream parties because they see none of them as offering a way forward that can bring fundamental improvement to the environment or other pressing issues. Unless they decide to waste their vote by supporting a fringe party, such as the Greens, they have no choice but to remain with one of the mainstream parties. Their votes could therefore be said to remain locked within the current context of competition. If sufficient public support for SP were to be available, a third party that adopted it would therefore have a great deal to gain. In a political environment where there is little or no differentiation between the policies of mainstream parties, voters will more readily focus upon aspects of difference. If the only significant difference was that the 'third' party had adopted SP, most of those environmentally-minded voters would be very attracted to it thus unlocking their votes and leaving them free to transfer from other mainstream parties to the 'third' party.

---

[2] See *Nature State and Economy*. Johnston points out: National Trust: 1,046,000 in 1981 to 2,032,000 in 1990. World Wide Fund for Nature: 12,000 to 247,000; Friends of the Earth: 18,000 to 110,000; Greenpeace: 30,000 to 372,000 over the same period.

Furthermore it would also, by the same token, attract much of the vote currently residing with fringe parties such as the Greens. Since it is clear in countries where representation is not proportional that such parties generally have no realistic chance of electoral success, their supporters would be attracted to a mainstream party that had adopted SP because they would perceive the double benefit of a policy that at last seeks to treat the root cause of global problems and the fact that their vote would no longer be wasted. Even though the numbers voting Green are relatively small, the combined number of *all* voters from *all* parties who care significantly for the environment and other issues that SP addresses would total a tidy sum which could make all the difference. This even more so, if the bulk of non-industrialised and developing nations had already adopted SP and public pressure around the world for adoption was mounting.

Let us now pause to consider what the additional circumstances might be if a third party had adopted it as a result of public support and the effect this could have on the main centre-left party.

SP: ADOPTION BY MAIN CENTRE-LEFT PARTIES

Virtually all western democracies are dominated by two parties, one centre-right, the other centre-left. However, although most centre-left parties have their roots in socialism and economic intervention, many have forsaken them, either because they have moved to the right in order to take the centre ground (as the UK Labour Party did in the 1997 election), or because they have become dependent on big business for funding. As has already been pointed out, the competitive context ruled by global free capital markets has irrevocably forced adherence by all mainstream parties to free market ideology and a domestic economic agenda characterised by a restricted welfare state and low public spending. The point will inevitably come, however, where traditional left-of-centre voters will not be able to reconcile their social democratic values with the worsening social and environmental consequences of unfettered global competition. Herein lies the dilemma of today's centre-left parties. Whilst they continue to pay lip service to traditional centre-left social concerns they are, in fact, forced to adopt a market and business-friendly stance by dint of the political demands of free markets. Ultimately, however, centre-left supporters will be unable to reconcile these two starkly divergent forces and the inevitable crisis of support will come.[3] If public support for a 'third' party were to grow significantly simply because it had adopted SP it would therefore also attract not only many who care for the environment, but also significant numbers of main centre-left party members and supporters who already feel deep unease with a party that has forsaken its roots. If the numbers so doing were large enough, the centre-left party would be caught on the horns of a nasty dilemma. It too would want to adopt SP to restore its support but would hesitate for fear of alienating one of its main sources of funding – big business. In such circumstances, clearly the level of public support for SP would already be very strong. In the end, faced with a choice between a loss of corporate funding or a loss of political support, it is not difficult to see what decision a main centre-left party must ultimately take. It would be forced to adopt SP or it could find itself relegated to third place and its main centre-left position usurped by its 'third' party rival.

Although admittedly many very large assumptions are made, one can see in principle how centre-left parties now in

---

[3] Tensions within the UK Labour Party are already beginning to show: see *The Independent*, 22.6.99 "Blair in Assault on Old Labour." And Old Labour's response: "Grassroots tell Blair to raise taxes" in *The Independent*, 24.6.99.

government in many countries might be persuaded (or gently coerced) into adopting SP. We can also see how corporate funding in politics could be eliminated. Indeed, in such a scenario, one would end up with both the main centre-left *and* the third party having adopted it. (The pressure this would exert on a centre-right party means their adoption of SP, which was hitherto regarded as totally unthinkable on ideological grounds, may then perhaps be cause for some reflection by its leadership).[4]

One draw-back to this approach is that a third party might see itself as being used merely as a 'stepping stone' to securing adoption of SP by the main centre-left party. For if the centre-left party adopted it to restore its traditional support, the third party would have gained little or nothing from the exercise. For this reason, it may not bother to adopt it in the first place. There is no certain answer to this conundrum. However, one would hope that, in taking the initiative, a third party could maintain the support of those voters it had drawn away from the centre-left party. Being seen to be the original party to adopt SP should imply to those voters that it would be the party best trusted to implement it. In any case, if public support could be developed to such a pitch that significantly influenced the 'swing' or 'floating vote' one mainstream party or another would be bound to adopt it if only for fear of one of its rivals doing so first. (And if that happened, all the other mainstream parties, even possibly centre-right ones, would be forced to follow.)

By not seeking to change the existing policies of mainstream parties but merely by asking them to 'add' or adopt SP in this subtle but effective way, we can also far more easily harness the vast majority of voters who remain

---

[4] Even today, the UK Conservatives are seeking to distance themselves from free market solutions, at least in the sphere of public services. See *The Independent* 28th April. Page 8. "Senior Tory quits as 'civil war' deepens".

environmentally disinterested. They in any case already vote, and will always vote, for one or other of the main-stream parties (if they bother to vote at all).

Since third parties are not always available in some democracies, two-party democracies are considered below as a further example of how differing approaches to obtaining adoption of SP could be envisaged. This describes a country in which only two parties dominate: one centre-left, one centre-right. Both are highly influenced by funding from big business and both share free-market ideology: in short, a seemingly hopeless situation.[5]

SP: TWO-PARTY DEMOCRACIES

Here, I am referring to countries such as the United States. Both parties together dominate the political scene dwarfing all other parties. Both, as far as I am aware, are significantly funded by big business or other sectional interests. The policies of both embrace free market ideology: all in all, a seemingly desperate state of affairs. In such cases, there is a number of possible strategies.

One would be for the SP lobbying group of that country to target the supporters, membership and leadership of the centre-left party (the US Democrats) to a point where the numbers that had adopted SP became high enough to force it to reduce to relative insignificance the amount of funding it received from big business. At the same time, the SP organisa-tion would also mount a broadly based campaign in the wider public domain. If the numbers of Democrat supporters adopting SP were high enough, adoption by the party might be a distinct possibility, particularly if public opinion and adoption of SP were already well advanced in other western countries.

[5] Were the Liberal Democrats to merge with New Labour, as some reports have suggested, the 'two-party democracy' approach would need to be taken also in the UK.

An alternative strategy might be for the SP lobbying group to persuade all its members, be they Republican or Democrat voters, to abstain from the electoral process altogether. The lobbying group would also seek adoption amongst the already large numbers abstaining from US elections. This should not be difficult. After all, there is little to choose between the two parties so not voting at all would make little difference. Members of the public who now support either Republicans or Democrats cannot do so honestly expecting any real difference when either party reaches Congress or the White House.

"At a time of rising citizen participation in environmental and public interest groups, less than half US citizens even bother to vote. ... At the 1994 Congressional elections when the Republicans gained a majority, only a third of those eligible to vote did so. ... One survey found that only ten per cent of those who voted thought their vote made a difference and only seventeen per cent thought the election was important."[6]

Why the low vote? Noam Chomsky explains:

"When the interests of the privileged and powerful are the guiding commitments of both political factions, people who do not share these interests tend to stay home."[7]

The reasons for abstaining would be two-fold; firstly, the ever-lower numbers of voters taking part in the electoral process would itself undermine the legitimacy of the government. This abstention *en masse* would also make a very public statement on the state of that nation. In the case of the US, such action would high-light to the world – and most of all to American citizens themselves – the falsehood of those who still believe it to be the world's beacon of democracy, freedom

[6] *Global Spin*. Sharon Beder. Green Books, 1997. Page 241.
[7] Quoted from: *The Compassionate Revolution*. David Edwards. Green Books, 1998.

and a healthy society. The United States, as the leading proponent of economic liberalism and the global market, has
perhaps the most divided society of all developed nations
including a prison population of truly gargantuan proportions. The erosion of middle class America has resulted in a
large underclass comprising all except the super-rich.[8] This
should be increasingly fertile ground for the SP lobbying
group to gather widespread support through abstention from
the electoral process.

Secondly, growing abstention would create a pool of
potential voters all of whom would be committed to SP and
ready to vote for any party that adopted it. The organising
body would also have made clear publicly that it will urge all
its members to support whichever of the two parties that
adopts SP first. It does not care which party does so, but
whichever is first counts. The other party, even if it adopts
only two days after the first, counts for nothing and will
receive no support by so doing. Provided that the research
done by the two parties demonstrates and confirms that the
numbers of people abstaining or otherwise having adopted
SP are sufficient to swing the outcome of an election in
either direction, they will, I suggest, be falling over themselves
to be first to adopt SP, regardless of funding from big business,
for fear of their rival doing so first. Indeed, the U.S.
Presidential election which took place in the autumn of 2000
where the outcome was hanging on just a few hundred votes
in Florida demonstrates the feasibility of this strategy. Once
SP has developed into a more established political force, the
existence in the key states of a relatively low, yet critical,
number of people who had adopted SP could result in either,
or even both, of the main presidential candidates adopting SP.

---

[8] US domestic public opinion already seems to recognise the adverse
effects of globalisation. See *Foreign Affairs* Vol. 78, No. 2. Page 30. *America
and Europe: Clash of the Titans?* By C. Fred Bergsten, director of the
Institute for International Economics.

Were this strategy to fail in spite of massive public support, perhaps because the influence of big business on both parties is too highly endemic, there remains open the option of the lobbying group and its supporters transforming themselves into a third political party. This would clearly be a last resort and might only be considered if adoption of SP in other countries was already very well advanced. In doing so, the new party should, I suggest, adopt a range of policies designed for the current competitive context that was virtually identical to those of either of the main parties. The reason for this, of course, would be to high-light the lack of perceptible difference between all three parties in terms of their approach to today's competitive world. It would also serve to reassure supporters that it was prepared to be as tough a competitive fighter in the current context as either of the two main parties. Whilst taking no chances in the current context of competition, the only party offering a plausible way out for the future would then be, naturally, the SP party. As such it should be capable of attracting many from both the other two parties as supporters would have nothing to lose by switching their support and everything to gain in a similar way to what has been described in relation to a traditional three-party democracy such as the UK.

Of course, the above scenarios are rather simplistic but, I suggest, feasible in principle. I therefore see the objective of persuading one or more mainstream parties to adopt SP as feasible in (pseudo-)democratic countries. It is also a way of exposing and ultimately eliminating the damaging intrusion of corporate influence and funding in politics. Naturally, being British, my experience is mainly of the UK electoral system; however, I suggest the above ideas could be successfully applied to any (pseudo-)democratic country. Each country would, of course, have to be looked at so the best individual strategy and timing can be worked out that suits its particular political circumstances.

SP AND GAINING PUBLIC SUPPORT

Now let us consider the all-important matter of actually gaining adequate public support. After all, without being able to mobilise the public in favour of SP, none of what has so far been suggested could occur. Yet again, in considering this, we must remember that adoption of SP by any member of the public or by a small business, church or other organisation has no effect whatsoever on their current views, policies or behaviour because implementation only occurs when it has been adopted by all nations.

In looking at gaining public support, it will be discussed in terms of a single democratic country. Naturally, what is discussed would be occurring in many such countries. For the moment, however, let us continue to take Britain as an example. Following on from our discussion above, whilst the UK SP lobbying organisation would be seeking adoption by anyone of any political leaning, it would privately have agreed upon a strategy of focusing primarily on 'third' party adoption. In gaining adequate support there are therefore two distinct aspects. First is the task of directly lobbying a 'third' party, its leadership, members and supporters and to seek their adoption. Second is the task of gathering widespread adoption of SP amongst the wider public. The UK SP lobbying organisation would organise itself accordingly, having a core group of lobbyists concentrating solely on a 'third' party – the Liberal Democrats - whilst the remainder address the wider public.

As far as the lobbying of a 'third' party's leadership, members and supporters is concerned, since only a single political party is identified, the target is very narrow. The task of the lobbying group is therefore greatly simplified. They know exactly who to look for so identifying and finding them will therefore be relatively easy. They need not dilute their efforts by trying to reach everybody but can instead *focus* on a narrow few. As far as individual 'third' party sup-porters are concerned, localised research could be carried out by simply noting which party's placards are displayed in people's front windows in the run-up to general or other elections. No doubt other more sophisticated methods could also be employed.

Another important factor is that they are asking members and supporters of a 'third' party to consider only *one single issue*. Since SP can only be implemented once all nations have adopted it, it has no effect on a political party's current range of policies. SP therefore offers no policies on health, educa-tion, nor on any other day to day issue, permitting 'third' party supporters to fully maintain their position on those issues. They need only consider the single issue of whether to adopt SP. Indeed, the simple question that 'third' party sup-porters (or indeed anybody) would have to ask themselves is:

> Given that I can maintain all my views and my support for my party and all of its current policies, would it be in my best interests to adopt SP, the measures of which would only be implemented when all nations do likewise?

Since they would have little if anything to lose by adoption, I suggest gaining their support should be relatively easy. It should be possible to demonstrate how simultaneous implementation means that all countries and major business-es will all be subject to exactly the same constraints. Most objections to policies arise from the potentially unpleasant effects of unilateral implementation. For example, the Conservatives will say that high-taxing Labour will make Britain uncompetitive thus leading to higher unemploy-ment.[9] Similarly, businesses usually resist greater environmen-tal or social regulation on the basis that it will increase their

---

[9] Or at least the Conservatives *used* to be able to say this about Labour until New Labour, through the political demands of global markets, adopted Conservative policies!

121

costs thus making them uncompetitive and causing unemployment. But if all countries are to implement the same taxes or regulations simultaneously under SP, issues of competitiveness and consequent unemployment simply do not arise. Furthermore, and crucially, global simultaneous implementation could allow the burden of any increased taxation to fall entirely on the corporate sector. In fact, the balance could be shifted such that personal taxes are reduced and corporate taxes correspondingly increased. Since no issue of competition arises, the only effect would be that shareholders would receive lower dividends than they do now and individuals would pay less tax than they do now. Furthermore, such a move should more than adequately provide for improved social services, health care, education, Basic/Citizen's Income, etc. Being spread across all major corporations, the impact of this additional taxation should not cause them any significant difficulties. In a general sense, transnational and other major corporations could thus be made to fulfil a genuinely beneficial role in the service of world society as a whole rather than solely in the service of a highly restricted number of shareholders as they do today.

Not seeking to change people's minds by trying to force a new political party upon them – and with it a whole range of day-to-day policies designed for the current context - but instead merely asking them to make the 'declaration of intent' that adopting SP represents, is also an extremely important factor when looking, now, at the task of gaining support from the wider public.

Even though the primary aim of the SP organising body would be adoption by a 'third' party, it should be remembered that SP is capable of adoption by almost *any* political party. It is also quite feasible that *more than one* party may have adopted it. This gives it something of a non-party-political character. Since SP also has no impact on the current competitive context it therefore requires no change of existing views or policies. This doubly enhances SP's non-party-political ethos. As such, anyone openly displaying their support for SP could not be identified with any specific political party. If one saw an SP car sticker on the back window of someone's car, for example, who could say for sure whether they were a Labour, Green, Liberal-Democrat or even a Conservative voter? This is extremely important because it would enable all sorts of organisations and individuals, from religious organisations to hospitals and from schools to rock stars, to support SP and to become involved in promoting it. Moreover it would allow them to do so openly and vocally. After all, they would risk no rejection or discrimination on party-political grounds. Existing environmental and charitable organisations as well as other NGOs could also lend their support.

SP's non-party-political approach can, perhaps, best be illustrated if one imagines a situation likely to occur in marginal constituencies in the run-up to a UK General Election. In these constituencies, candidates quite often become Members of Parliament by a margin of a mere handful of votes. When adoption of SP develops in those constituencies to the point where a critical number of voters - perhaps just a few hundred – had adopted and were willing to vote for *any* candidate that adopts, one could foresee the local SP organisation writing to each candidate in advance of the election telling them of this fact and asking them to carefully consider whether they, too, would like to adopt. In such circumstances, it is rather difficult to see how any of the mainstream candidates could avoid doing so and they would have to reply accordingly or face the high likelihood of defeat. It would then only remain for the local SP organisation to advise all those candidates that it will be delighted to confirm their adoption on the lawn outside the House of Commons in the presence of the national media. One can then imagine the newsworthiness and novelty of a policy that, perhaps for the first time in history, had been adopted by every mainstream candidate, if not by all candidates, across the entire political spectrum. News of such a novel phenomenon is then likely not only to spread rapidly and generate a vibrant national debate that focuses on SP, but it will also give added impetus and encouragement to the adoption campaign elsewhere. Indeed, in today's boring and vacuous political environment, I suggest this kind of news will travel fast.

SP's non-party-political and all-inclusive ethos thus accepts people for what they are without judging them and promotes national and international unity. By being blind to current political differences, to rich or poor, to right or left, SP lets bygones be bygones. It enables people to aspire to and work towards a new way of life without risking their survival in the current context of competition. It similarly allows politicians to adopt without risking marginalisation. It allows us all openly to share and discuss our dreams and desires for a new way of life – a new *quality* of life – more compatible with human nature and with Nature itself. This non-judgmental and non-party political approach which *unites* people rather than *dividing* them could therefore prove a powerful and decisive force.

From a political campaigning point of view, another factor to be remembered is that events would, over the years of a campaign, be playing right into the hands of those advocating SP. For as the vortex of global competition gathers further force, regrettably, social, economic and environmental decay can only continue to worsen and therefore support can only grow. As the march through 'emptiness' proceeds, events can only encourage growing numbers around the world to join it.

Finally, we have to ask: what alternatives to SP does the public have? The only alternatives on offer are either the false hope or dream that the resources of high technology that serve the capitalist system might somehow find a solution for us, or the view that things will only improve when it is forced upon us by global economic, social or environmental collapse.

In seeing no way out of our current problems, many are resorting to local solutions, especially those in more rural communities, by seeking to de-link themselves from the national and international economy by developing their own self-reliant economies with the help of informal local currencies (LETS), credit unions and greater self-reliance in energy and food production. Many such initiatives are thriving albeit on a relatively small scale.[10] However, even if such welcome and unorthodox efforts were to become widespread, they do nothing to alter the powers of a distrustful and suspicious state to interfere or legislate against them. Furthermore, the vast majority of the population living in urban areas is likely − like it or not − to remain highly dependent on the mainstream economy. In any case, in the event of widespread collapse of the mainstream economy, neither those dependent on it nor those de-linked from it are likely to escape the inevitably chaotic and possibly horrific effects. Small scale solutions, whilst pointing the way to a more ecological lifestyle of the future and being absolutely valid in themselves, do not constitute a real alternative for most of us.

In the absence of SP, by far the most immediate form of collapse will, I suggest, be social. As corporations consolidate and employ ever more sophisticated labour-saving technology in their battle to maintain competitiveness and increase profits, so the result will be increasing unemployment and social decay. History has shown that this translates into an

---

[10] A comprehensive survey of such initiatives is given in *Short Circuit - Strengthening Local Economies for Security in an Unstable World*. Richard Douthwaite, Green Books, 1996.

increasing shift of public political support towards far-right parties, the dire and horrific human consequences of which we have witnessed before. We can wait for that collapse to happen, or we can try to prevent it happening by pursuing the alternative political choice that SP represents.

As a final comment on gaining public support, David Korten's experiences, amongst others, should be borne in mind:

> "...each time I prepare to speak to a new group I invariably have a nervous feeling that what I have to say will be rejected out of hand in a world committed to growth, big business, and deficit financing. Yet the usual response is an outpouring of affirmation from people who express their relief and pleasure at the unusual experience of having their own experience affirmed in a public forum. Getting the difficult and unpleasant truth out on the table for discussion is a necessary step toward action. Whereas fear of the unknown may immobilize us, the truth empowers us to act."[11]

So, whilst we may think we are waiting for the people, surely growing numbers are already waiting for us. Indeed, *openness* about the problems of the capitalist system and the world problems we face is crucial. A major objective of the adoption process is for those who have adopted SP openly to advertise the fact, thus challenging others to do likewise. The concept of universal adoption means that everyone who has heard of SP knows their adoption to be valuable as part of a world-wide process. That feeling of the personal value of each and every individual as part of a world-wide adoption campaign cannot be overestimated. All people of the world will thus be able to take part in solving our two world problems – two fundamental and deeply human problems. As the march through 'emptiness' proceeds and gathers force, its

---

[11] *When Corporations Rule the World*. David Korten. Kumarian Press Inc. and Berrett-Koehler Publishers, 1995.

spiritual significance to all humanity will become ever more evident. SP's non-party-political character and non-judgmental ethos allows this to happen. Everyone can therefore play their part, but if they choose not to adopt, they should expect to have a good reason.

Like fighting over sandwiches, once a certain critical mass of participants has adopted the proposal of co-operation, the rest tend to follow in fairly short order. I therefore see the gaining of adequate public support as feasible and, dare I say, possibly easier than we might think.

7. SP: Adoption by Non-Industrial & Developing Nations

> "Security, happiness and peaceful relations are desired by all. Until, however, the Great Powers, in collaboration with the little nations, have solved the economic problem and realized that the resources of the earth belong to no one nation but to humanity as a whole, there will be no peace."[1]

ADOPTION BY DEVELOPING COUNTRIES

Many such countries have experienced at first hand what are, at best, the mixed effects of "Structural Adjustment Programs" (SAPs) imposed by developed nations through the IMF and the World Bank:

> "There is considerable evidence that the neo-liberal programmes, and SAPs in particular, are not effective in bringing about economic development, either when economic development is defined narrowly in terms of economic growth or when it is defined more broadly to include other aspects of social well-being."[2]

Successive waves of 'third world development' or 'structural adjustment' all have one self-defeating aspect in common: that they encourage the development of *dependency* rather than *self-reliance*. This has continued for about 50 years under one guise or another yet still 60 percent of the world's population live on less than $2 per day.

[1] *Problems of Humanity.* Alice A. Bailey. Lucis Publishing Co, 1947.
[2] *Neo-Liberalism or Democracy?* Arthur MacEwan, Zed Books, 1999.

Some blinkered economists argue for what they see as the overwhelming benefits of current modes of investment in such countries. They point, for example, to Indonesia which had a gross national product (GNP) lower than Nigeria in 1965, yet until just before the Asian financial crisis boasted a GNP three times that of struggling Nigeria. However, as Jeff Gates points out: "At every turn, however, we are faced not only with the question of what causes development but also how to measure it. Indonesia for instance, has been a Southeast Asian success story for more than twenty years, its economy (until recently) the envy of countries throughout the region. However, much of that success was generated by selling off its nonrenewable mineral wealth, clear-cutting its tropical forests and exhausting its topsoil with overly intensive farming."[2]

A further problem with such development approaches is that they benefit relatively few people as Jeff Gates also observes: "...though resource-rich Brazil has enjoyed an annual growth of 7 to 8 percent, it has one of the world's most dramatic income inequalities, with more than 40 percent mired in poverty. In 1960, the top 20 percent of Brazilians received thirty times more income than the bottom 20 percent. By 1989, that gap had grown to sixty times."[3]

Yet with all the evidence that now exists to show that Structural Adjustment simply does not work, the IMF and the World Bank still insist there is no alternative; that poorer countries would have been even poorer without SAPs and that their failure must be due to other reasons. That failure is, they often say, not the IMF's fault but the fault of poor-country governments who are either corrupt or failed to implement the IMF's prescriptions rigorously enough. But here again we see the 'mind-set of competition' at work. The flawed thought-process of the IMF and

---

[3] *The Ownership Solution.* Jeff Gates, Penguin Books, 1998.

the World Bank runs, I suggest, something like this: "Globalisation and the free market are natural and inevitable, so competition is inevitable. The better a nation competes in the global market and the more 'market access' it has, the richer it will become. Since SAPs and 'market access' make a country more competitive, so SAPs will make them richer. So SAPs are not bad – how can they be bad? No, since they make a country more competitive, they must be good. So good, we can also feel we are fulfilling our pledge as a world institution to further the cause of poverty reduction." Matching this flawed thought-process, a similar thinking lies behind the steady decrease in foreign aid provided by rich countries to poorer ones: "Competition makes us richer so, by the same token, glob-alisation and SAPs will make poor countries richer. So why bother with foreign aid? We don't need it and in any case freely donated aid would be a distortion of competition. Since competition is good, any distortion of it must be bad. (In fact, it would be a kind of protectionism.) So we must decrease it or do away with it altogether." It is this funda-mentally flawed mind-set, I suggest, which underlies much of current 'development' thinking and it all stems from the blind acceptance of globalisation - and therefore competi-tion – as being inevitable and exclusively beneficial.

This also explains why the elite, in the form of politi-cians, the IMF, the World Bank and the WTO, continue to get away with SAPs or other 'spun' versions of the same policy in spite of growing protest against their policies. For if it is tacitly accepted, both by the multi-lateral institutions and by those who oppose them, that the free movement of capital and cor-porations – i.e. global competition – cannot be re-regulated, the inevitable effect is that both sides remain locked in an endless loop of lame excuses on the one hand, and (some-times violent) protest on the other, with neither side able to find a way out because they are both, effectively, subject to an over-arching paradigm of global competition neither can influence. They and the millions of poverty-stricken at the receiving end of neo-liberal policies are all, therefore, victims of the continuing quasi-dictatorship of competition and of the thought-process that accompanies it. Therefore, until the multi-lateral institutions, the politicians and, indeed, the pro-testers are able to see that the free movement of capital and corporations is neither inevitable nor exclusively beneficial, and until they recognise SP (or something similar) as a poten-tial solution, the disastrous consequences of that mind-set seem destined to remain with us.

Be that as it may, adoption of SP by developing countries nevertheless presents a distinct problem. On the one hand the effects of foreign investment have been at best mixed and have wrought considerable damage to the environment. On the other, these countries, or at least the upper elite tier of their populations, have tasted what they see as the sweet fruits of industrial development. Many such countries, particularly in south-east Asia, have major corporations already domiciled in their territories who could be expected to resist adoption.

"...TNCs have concentrated their FDI [foreign direct invest-ment] in a small number of developing countries often because they had authoritarian governments and were judged to be reliable 'client' states."[4]

The key to adoption of SP, however, lies in the growth of democracy (albeit of the 'pseudo' variety) that economic development has brought with it:

"Albeit in the highly specialized form of party contest, repre-sentative democracy has continued its global spread, from India to Chile, from South Africa to the Philippines, an

[4] *Big Business, Poor Peoples.* John Madeley. Zed Books, 1999.
[5] *Politics in an Antipolitical Age.* Geoff Mulgan. Polity Press, 1994. Page 8.

extraordinary global reach comparable only to that of capitalist ideas and institutions."[5]

Whilst scope for reform within existing (pseudo-) democracies has been severely narrowed by the dictates of global free markets, they have also paradoxically served to extend democracy itself.[6] To the extent that developing countries are democratic, the 80 percent of their populations largely by-passed by economic development need to be mobilised to force adoption. This sounds highly simplistic, but as part of a well-publicised world public movement for adoption, and with committed work at grass-roots level, it should be possible to mobilise public opinion to obtain adoption by mainstream political parties in a similar way to advanced democratic countries. After all, civil society movements for change are increasing in strength partly as a consequence of neo-liberal policies:

> "Experiences in many … countries provide … examples of the basic process by which the organizations of civil society can provide small wedges that can enlarge political space … These organizations range from the long-standing labour unions to the newly burgeoning environmental protection organizations, … from peasant cooperatives attempting to protect their livelihoods to student or parent associations dealing with the quality of the schools."[7]

Non-democratic developing countries pose the greatest difficulty, however, and in particular where governments are supported in power by advanced countries to assure supplies of natural resources and to maintain corporate profits. Such countries are often forced into agreements not always in their best interests:

---

[6] For example, China's integration into the global economy and its imminent entry into the WTO are expected to strengthen pressure for a transition to democracy in China. See *The Independent*, 16th November 1999, page 16.

[7] *Neo-Liberalism or Democracy?* Arthur MacEwan, Zed Books, 1999.

"In theory the WTO is a democratic one-country, one-vote organisation, and if developing countries stand together in Seattle they can get the round of trade talks they want. In practice, however, many receive aid from Western governments, and will try to avoid upsetting them if they possibly can. Developing countries may be persuaded to join a 'consensus' that is hardly in their interests."[8]

Up to the end of the Cold War, western support for such countries was successfully justified in the interests of keeping communism at bay. But with the Cold War now ended, this argument has evaporated allowing the real reasons to become clear. Naturally, where governments of non-democratic developing countries are in collusion with corporate or western interests, adoption of SP would be unlikely. There are, however, three points to be borne in mind:

Firstly, there remain at least some developing nations not subject to such collusion who could therefore be persuaded to adopt. Those that do so would then serve to highlight the reasons why some others have chosen not to. This would therefore bring these issues out into the open resulting in those developing countries that have adopted setting a moral challenge to the others to cease their collusion. This would be important if only to better inform world public opinion and so create a sense of moral challenge amongst developing nations themselves.

Secondly, the availability to such nations of the inward investment provided by the Tobin and Development taxes would demonstrate the practice of attracting inward investment by allowing their territory to be stripped of its natural resources by foreign corporations as completely unnecessary. Currently, these nations are offered little alternative if they want to pursue economic development. The only

[8] From an article by John Madeley appearing in the *Church Times*, November 1999.

choice open to them today is to take on massive debts which are, of course, only available on the condition that they submit to Structural Adjustment which involves damaging financial deregulation and trade liberalisation. Funds raised from the Development Tax, on the other hand, would effectively be donated free and would, therefore, offer these countries an infinitely more attractive alternative which it would be incumbent upon them to accept.

Thirdly, a better informed public opinion in advanced countries will put increasing pressure on western politicians and corporations to cease their collusion with client developing countries. Indeed, once the adoption process is well advanced, it is feasible that some parties in government in Western countries may already have adopted SP (as outlined in the previous chapter) whilst the governments of the developing countries they are supporting may not yet have done so. This would put extreme pressure on those advanced countries not only to cease their collusion but, instead, to start encouraging those nations to adopt.

If the adoption process were already well advanced and adoption by the poorest non-industrial nations as well as by some advanced democratic countries had been achieved, the remaining non-democratic developing nations would then represent a rump of states where adoption remained outstanding. These countries might then additionally require, regrettably, some coercion as a last resort. This could take the form of economic sanctions or consumer boycotts or other measures. These are discussed in greater detail in chapter 8 but it should be stressed that their use should be contemplated only as a very last resort. Wherever possible, force of argument and goodwill should prevail.

ADOPTION BY NON-INDUSTRIALISED COUNTRIES

The poorest countries, however, remain largely ignored by the world economy and foreign investors. Having 20 percent of the world's people, these countries receive a derisory 0.2 percent of the world's commercial lending. In addition, their share of world trade fell, between 1960 and 1990, from an already low 4 percent to less than 1 percent.

The primary function of adoption of SP by non-industrialised or less-developed nations would be to signify the denial of their territories to corporations seeking a haven to avoid the constraints of SP. Obviously this is vital, for without it global co-operation could not be assured. In exchange for denying their territories to TNCs, they would benefit from the inward investment provided debt-free by the Tobin and Development Taxes. In considering the prospects for their adoption, the poorest countries have few if any major corporations or institutions domiciled in their countries and, when the time came, implementation would therefore be unlikely to involve much practical change if any. Given that SP also includes the complete cancellation of Third World debt, these nations can therefore only stand to gain by its eventual implementation. To receive the massive inward investment generated by the Tobin and Development Taxes, their fulfillment of the condition of ensuring the direct application of those funds to their neediest people can similarly only be of benefit. After all, the volume of funds made available by a direct tax on major corporations would dwarf the derisory 0.2 percent currently achieved. It would also make redundant the rather dubious practice by governments of advanced countries providing 'overseas development aid' which has often been conditional upon arms purchases or the awarding of commercial contracts.

Many of the poorest countries are also non-democratic. This would allow national SP lobbying organisations to approach governments directly to seek adoption without the need to go through lengthy democratic processes. Where corporate interests represent a block to adoption, to the extent that the corporations concerned could be identified, the possibility of applying added pressure through consumer boycotts could prove effective. Within the framework of a widespread international adoption campaign, the pressure applied to governments or corporations could be quite considerable. Each country would, of course, need to be looked at individually to assess prospects for adoption.

Where democracies are involved it may, to a large extent, be possible to quicken democratic processes towards adoption because, as I have said, implementation would involve little, if any, practical change for those countries. As such, there would be little or no downside over which to deliberate.

REASSURANCE AND SETTING THE EXAMPLE

In adopting SP, poorer countries would be setting a crucial example. On one level, as I have pointed out, their adoption is largely academic since eventual implementation would involve no significant change other than an in-flow of freely donated funds. On another level, adoption is crucial because it would challenge richer countries (as well as some developing countries) to follow their example. Indeed, their adoption would set an example to the whole world. For it would demonstrate the need for more developed and advanced industrialised countries to treat the *cause* of the problems they have inflicted on the world rather than only the symptoms. Global warming, deforestation, soil erosion, rampant population growth, infectious diseases and refugees are, after all, merely symptoms of the problem. It is destructive competition and its attendant lack of spiritual values that is the cause. Industrialised countries like to focus on symptoms because they largely manifest themselves in poor countries, a fact that has proved convenient, because it implies that these symptoms are somehow problems poor nations are responsible for and should deal with by themselves.

All the while no example is set by poorer countries as to *how* the rich industrialised countries should solve these problems, industrialised and more developed nations can continue to get away with making (and breaking) more and more promises with respect to restricting global warming emissions, poverty reduction and other such targets. Conversely, if poor countries were to adopt SP, until universal adoption were achieved, logically the focus of international pressure and challenge could only remain where it belongs: firmly on industrialised and more developed countries to follow the example of the poor nations of the South by adopting SP. This, I suggest, would mark a fundamental change of emphasis in North - South relations: a *qualitative* change that would put significant pressure on the industrialised countries at least to consider the implications of adoption.

At the same time, adoption by non–industrial and developing nations would have another crucial and important effect. This would be to reassure the advanced or more-developed nations by reducing their fear. For it is primarily fear that haunts the rich nations today and drives them to exclude the poor: fear for their continued wealth at the expense of the poor. In considering whether they too should adopt SP, the rich developed nations of the North would be assured that major corporations could not expect to evade regulation by moving their domicile to Southern developing or non–industrial nations. This act of selfless generosity by the nations of the South to remove fear amongst nations of the North would therefore not only make it much easier for the

Northern countries to follow their example, it would demonstrate that it is also incumbent upon them to do so. In this way, the South would be putting pressure on the North to adopt SP but, at the same time, would also be offering it an olive branch.

For practical purposes, it may be that some poor nations are regrettably in such desperate chaos that they have no government capable of considering adoption. Such nations would in any case be unlikely to provide an inviting domicile for transnational corporations and the need for their adoption could perhaps be overlooked. It would, however, be a shame to do so for these nations are the very ones that have suffered most. Every effort should therefore be made to secure their adoption of SP, if only for the symbolic and publicity value it would have.

8. The International Simultaneous Policy Organisation

"This is no mystical or impractical program; it does not work through the processes of exposing, undermining or attack; it emphasises the new politics, i.e., politics which are based upon the principle of bringing about right human relations. Between the exploited and the exploiting, the warmongers and the pacifists, the masses and the rulers, this group of men [and women] of goodwill will stand in their organized millions, taking no side, demonstrating no partisan spirit, fomenting no political or religious distur-bance and feeding no hatreds. They will not be a negative body but a positive group, interpreting the meaning of right human relations, standing for the oneness of humanity and for practical, but not theoretical, brotherhood."[1]

Moving on to the structure and activities of ISPO itself, it is an organisation growing in numbers and its influence is extending to many countries. The prime initial objective has been to convince people of the need for, feasibility of, and indeed the plain *common sense* of global simultaneous imple-mentation against a background of a world steadily sinking in a downward spiral of destructive competition. Once people see this, they often concentrate their active efforts on the work of ISPO, seeing it as the most essential work they can possibly contribute towards the goal of a healthy and peaceful world. Indeed, so powerful is the idea to those who see this, it takes on a conviction and urgency all its own. The

---

[1] *Problems of Humanity.* Alice A. Bailey. Lucis Publishing Co, 1947.

emphasis, therefore, has been on spreading *the idea* of SP rather than on discussing what its actual measures might be. Indeed, as has been pointed out, SP is really a *vehicle* through which its aims can be achieved. In articulating a blueprint for how the vital transition from our current crisis to that new world can be made in a secure and responsible way, SP provides a clean sheet of paper upon which we can together design a new world of international community in which our diverse cultures and peoples can live in peace and cooperation with one another and in a manner compatible with the natural environment.

By the time it becomes necessary to define the measures of SP, ISPO will have become a large and positive group of people from all over the world having the task of melding their own solutions into a world policy: the Simultaneous Policy. Indeed, it will not be for the leaders of ISPO to prescribe what the measures of SP should be. Instead, ISPO's task in terms of policy making will be to facilitate an open and democratic process through which all those who adopt SP can, if they wish, play a part in developing its detailed measures. In the context of global co-operation they will need to remember that almost anything can be achieved. As far as possible, its measures will need to be politically neutral and focus upon keeping risks low.

Examples of the kind of measures ISPO should seek out in formulating SP measures are those consistent with different cultural and religious attitudes to "livelihood". One such measure could be the broadening of ownership. In *The Ownership Solution*, Jeff Gates shows how wider ownership within capitalism would result in a broader sharing of prosperity and an increasing connectedness amongst us as well as between us and our environment. More importantly, employee ownership finds favour amongst both political left and right and it therefore exemplifies the politically neutral measures SP should consist of. Beyond these alterations to ownership patterns, however, their highest form is that of decentralised common ownership as exemplified by the Scott Bader Commonwealth and this should, I believe, be the ultimate target.[2]

Were the proposal of a 'corporation tax for equity' swap proposed earlier in this book thought to be of merit, ISPO would need to define the details of who the "special directors" would be, how they would be appointed, what size of corporation would be affected and how financial institutions would be treated, etc.

As far as campaigning is concerned, national SP organisations are starting to analyse and assess the political circumstances of their individual countries with a view to commencing the actual work of lobbying the public and mainstream parties. This will, however, require considerable manpower; a requirement which could in certain cases be fulfilled, I respectfully suggest, by the Green parties and their supporters. In countries or elections having a non-proportional, 'first past the post' system, it is clear that fringe parties such as the Greens have little, if any, realistic chance of being elected to government. As we have seen, to offer the public a fringe party (and with it, a whole range of policies designed for the current competitive context), has become substantially futile under that system. Although managing sometimes to lessen the damage, it is clear that the Greens cannot change the overall direction. Furthermore, maintaining their status as a political party in those circumstances can sometimes have the unfortunate result of splitting the centre-left vote thus allowing an even more business-friendly party to be elected (as is said to have occurred in the U.S. Presidential election in

---

[2] In seeking patterns for broader ownership, there is a distinct danger that employee share ownership serves merely to turn employees or others into 'mini-capitalists'. It is for this reason that I believe the model of the Scott Bader Commonwealth to provide a far better solution.

2000). So Green parties should earnestly begin to question the value of maintaining their electoral ambitions in these cases. How much more effective could they be by pledging to vote for whichever of the mainstream parties adopts SP instead of splitting the centre-left vote? Might not the SP approach ultimately offer not only a better chance of success but also the prospect of far more meaningful reform?

Even in the highly unlikely event that Green parties were to come to power in countries like the UK or the USA, we should ask ourselves what - under the prevailing conditions of internationally mobile capital - they could actually achieve? Even under Germany's more favourable electoral system where the Greens share power they are plagued by the dilemmas of the current competitive context:

> "Germany's Greens, who have seen their popularity slump since coming into power as part of Chancellor Schroeder's coalition government, were locked in a bitter internal debate at a party congress in Erfurt last weekend. Party members are outraged that their leaders have been forced into humiliating climbdowns over issues dear to their hearts, such as their proposals to reform Germany's strict nationality laws. 'We have to combine our visions with what it is actually possible to achieve,' Germany's most high-profile Green, Foreign Minister Joschka Fischer, told the conference, but his speech was heard in stony silence."[3]

> "The rift in the six-month-old coalition of Social Democrats and Greens grew even wider last week, following an outspoken attack by Juergen Trittin, the Green environment minister, on the government of which he is part. 'Red-Green as a reform project is dead,' he told Stern magazine. Trittin blames Chancellor Schroeder for bowing to pressure from German business."[4]

---

[3] *The Week.* 13th March 1999, issue 195.
[4] *The Week.* 27th March 1999, issue 197.

Green party leaders inevitably find the measures they would like to introduce simply cannot be implemented without risking their nation's competitiveness. They therefore remain largely hamstrung in their efforts with potentially destructive consequences for their supporters who didn't vote Green to accept endless compromises. In reaching a position of power they and any other Green party will only find themselves - like any political party - confined to policies that must necessarily fall within the narrow parameters of competition: at the beck and call of transnational corporations and subject to the strangle-hold of neo-liberal policies dictated by global financial markets. Logically, therefore, the only circumstances in which Green parties could truly implement their manifestos would be once they had gained power in virtually every country in the world: i.e. when competition between nation states had been eliminated. Until then, they inevitably remain trapped in the competitive context and can do little more than any other party to protect society or the environment.[5]

The key challenge consequently confronting the Green movement, the political left and traditional, 'one-nation' Conservatives or their counterparts in other countries is to accept that unless they come to power in the vast majority of countries in the world and stay there long enough to be able to coordinate their policies, their desires to re-direct the world on to the path of sustainability will be frustrated. Naturally I am not suggesting that Green Parties should refrain immediately, or even soon, from contesting elections wherever non-proportional systems prevail, for at the time of writing the SP approach remains untested and unproven. Nevertheless, if the arguments put forward in this book are

---

[5] Indeed, the need to make their policies conform to current context realities and to avoid scaring off wary voters explains why the manifestos of Green Parties around the world are today so timid.

generally accepted, some reappraisal of their overall strategy would seem appropriate. And in considering that strategy, surely the above-mentioned experience of the German Green Party should provide some guidance.

For instead of continuing along a path likely to be fraught with on-going dilemmas and damaging compromises, Green parties could make use of the SP 'technology' to radically and imaginatively re-think their strategies. In elections under proportional representation systems where there is some hope of them being voted into office, they could make it clear that their manifesto will restrict itself only to those policies which can be implemented unilaterally. Because *that*, realistically, is all they will have a chance of implementing in any case. And for those policies which require global simultaneous implementation, they could, I respectfully suggest, adopt SP. Furthermore, if their support is needed by another party to form a coalition government, they should make their co-operation conditional upon their coalition partner adopting SP. In this way, their manifesto of policies for the current competitive context could be less radical and would be much more realistic and achievable. It would also make co-operation with a coalition partner easier to agree. Because SP can only be implemented when all nations do likewise, their coalition partner would also have nothing politically to lose by adopting SP and everything to gain. Furthermore, Green Party supporters could end their dilemma by making the clear distinction between those policies which can be implemented unilaterally and those which can only be implemented under SP. This far more appropriate strategy would, I suggest, at last allow Green supporters to make sense of their party's proper political role in a globalized world and thereby restore and broaden the party's appeal both to its own supporters and to the wider electorate. Depending on the electoral system prevailing in European, national or local elections, they could also be more selective about which elections to fight thus concentrating valuable campaigning resources. Moreover, they could use the SP 'technology' to help them develop a truly coherent global strategy. In this way, they could give themselves a more realistic and meaningful role in today's competitive world while equally making a far more dramatic impact on global politics as a whole either by enhancing their chances of outright electoral victory or by forcing would-be coalition partners to adopt SP.

As support for SP continues to gather pace, it is my hope that Green parties and others with similar objectives might take up the challenge of spearheading the SP adoption campaign. If they chose to do so, they could give it the benefit of their considerable and committed experience. And by co-operating strategically together with national SP lobbying organisations, they could play an enormously valuable role as campaigners, united around a single world policy and could rapidly spread adoption as they go while enhancing their party's support. Even if they choose not to re-think their current strategy, I suggest they could at least 'back both horses' by adopting SP.

As far as ISPO's symbol or logo is concerned, it was decided at ISPO's inauguration that it would be based on what I refer to as the "Schumacher Egg". It depicts the Earth trapped inside an egg but in the process of breaking out of its shell - a powerful symbol of both world-community and re-birth. Or one could see it as depicting the earth trapped within a restrictive and suffocating shell of destructive competition from which it must break out in order to survive: a vision of global unity, transformation and liberation. It is these visions and the thinking of Fritz Schumacher that has helped to inspire SP and it is therefore appropriate that SP's logo, as it appears on the front cover of this book, should be known as the 'Schumacher Egg'.

ISPO'S POWERS OVER GOVERNMENTS

ISPO's aim is to create for itself a public image not dissimilar to the Nobel Prize Committee. No one, I think, would be predisposed to question the international high regard in which this organisation is held, nor the impact and prestige of winning the Nobel Prize, particularly for Peace. ISPO is aiming for much the same image in the eyes of the public, of business leaders and of politicians around the world. ISPO cannot (and should not) have power as such over governments but it will, like the Nobel Committee, have the power to confer prestigious awards upon individuals, companies, organisations, political parties or governments. Unlike the Nobel Committee (so far as I know), ISPO will also have the power to remove them. Therefore, just as receiving an ISPO award will eventually be highly prestigious and attract much publicity, its removal can hardly be seen by a worldwide public holding ISPO in such high regard as anything less than a total condemnation of the action that caused its removal.

It is therefore envisaged that ISPO or national SP organisations will award a bronze Schumacher Egg to any individual, organisation, political party, dictator, school or government, etc who adopts SP in full. If any organisation or political party holding the bronze egg renounced SP or sought to deviate in any way from its full terms they would automatically have the award withdrawn, naturally attracting all the same publicity accorded them when they received it. As such, there would be little point in anyone seeking to adopt SP unless they intended to stick to it. Such an approach, I believe, expresses well Schumacher's principle of 'The Middle Axiom':

> "Neither the soft method of government by exhortation nor the tough method of government by instruction meets the requirements of the case. What is required is something in between, a middle axiom, an order from above which is yet not quite an order."[6]

In this way, ISPO could be said to be giving an order to national governments and political parties which is yet not quite an order. It is finely balanced but it should prove to be a formula acceptable to both voters and governments alike.

Silver Schumacher Eggs will be awarded to those who additionally contribute significantly to campaigning for the adoption of SP. This might be individuals who accomplish great things persuading other individuals to adopt. It may be small businesses that persuade others. It may be large corporations who see the approaching disaster and so seek to persuade their competitors by setting an example. Or it may be governments, or the UN who use their power to influence other nations to adopt SP. More than one silver egg might be awarded during the campaign reflecting the long and difficult process it will undoubtedly represent.

As for the Gold Schumacher Egg, well, I suppose we would all get one when global adoption has been achieved and implementation proceeds.[7] An awards scheme of this kind should not be necessary once public support for ISPO becomes adequately strong. However, symbolic gestures are sometimes useful.

This gesture of awarding Schumacher Eggs, combined with the crucial fact that politicians' electoral success would in any case have become dependent upon their adoption of SP, ensures that political parties and governments will have no scope or power to vary SP's terms or measures. Indeed, matters of global policy will have been taken completely out of their hands. But since support for the measures of SP derives directly and solely from those who have adopted it, politicians who decide to adopt as a result of that public electoral support or pressure will be seen to have done so entirely

---

[6] *Small is Beautiful.* E.F. Schumacher. Abacus, 1974.

[7] Schumacher Eggs would naturally not actually be made of these metals - the 'metal' is purely symbolic!

democratically. Unlike other NGOs or 'pressure groups' who are often accused of failing to engage in established democratic processes, ISPO and SP *work through the existing political system* and cannot therefore be accused of any such failure.

Insofar as SP might contain the 'corporation tax for equity swap' proposed in this book whereby governments would be entitled to appoint 'special directors' to the boards of major corporations, another important aspect concerns the independence of those directors. If they were purely appointed by governments, or by the corporations themselves, a very real danger of a conflict of interest would arise. It is therefore proposed that the special directors be responsible only to ISPO. However, lists of candidates would be provided by ISPO to governments so they could select candidates, preferably in consultation with the corporation concerned. I believe that if public opinion and adoption of SP ever got to the point where universal adoption appeared likely, I doubt governments would be too concerned about this 'benevolent intrusion' into their field of powers. A further argument for this approach is that responsibility of the "special directors" to ISPO would ensure, as far as possible, that a uniform and even-handed approach is taken on a world-wide basis. A further question is whether enough sufficiently qualified people could be found to fill all these special board room positions. However, I believe there are plenty of socially and environmentally conscious managers around. As David Korten has said, the problem is the current system which makes it difficult for them to survive.[8] In a new era of co-operation, however, I believe many such managers will want to come forward to fill these challenging and crucially important positions.

Yet a further aspect of power over governments is one that could arise in the later stages of campaigning. It could, for example, be envisaged that a few countries might remain

---

[8] *When Corporations Rule the World.* David Korten. Kumarian Press Inc. and Berrett-Koehler Publishers, 1995.

completely resistant to SP in spite of the majority. In such a case, the possibility of applying economic sanctions might assist. (The sanctions which were applied and were an important factor leading to the abolition of apartheid in South Africa spring to mind.) Here, however, whilst ISPO might call for such sanctions, it would be governments who would decide. By that stage, I suggest world public opinion would be so strongly in favour of SP that governments would be under great pressure to apply them. Such action should, however, only be contemplated as a last resort.

A final aspect of power over governments might be the growing power of those supporting SP to exert influence over major corporations, and thereby indirectly over governments, by exercising their power of purchasing boycott. In the latter stages of campaigning in each country, this may also prove a very useful tool. Even recently it was successfully used in preventing the sinking of the disused Brent Spar oil platform into the Atlantic ocean. Such action could prove particularly potent in two-party democracies such as the US where funding from big business is rife and, as I have argued, adoption therefore presents particular difficulties.[9] Consumer action today remains but a fleeting glimpse of the power of the people and is used only in the context of single emotive issues. Focused instead on a sustained and organised campaign for the adoption of SP, however, such action could have a remarkable and decisive impact.

In a sense, ISPO might come to be regarded as the world's "conscience". Jeff Gates identifies the need for such a conscience in respect of making capitalism more inclusive by broadening ownership.[10] I suggest what is needed is a broader

---

[9] Similar protests against the use of 'sweat-shop' labour from low-cost countries took place in universities in the USA against Nike Corp. See *The Guardian*, 25th June 1999: "Nike on the run as sit-ins spread across the US".

[10] *The Ownership Solution.* Jeff Gates. Penguin, 1998.

world conscience embodied in an organisation encompassing not only ownership but also environmental, ecological, developmental and many other issues. ISPO would thus act as the world's good conscience – for we all need one – influencing both people and governments on all these issues and, at the same time, being influenced by them. Like all well-integrated humans, conscious and sub-conscious parts of our personality serve to balance and moderate one another.

We saw, in 1648, how the Treaty of Westphalia created the 'society of nation states' which unleashed more than three centuries of competitive chaos culminating in its zenith as expressed by the global market. SP would at last bring that era to a close by giving birth to a genuine 'community of nation states'; a community in which the immense national and global economic, social and ecological challenges that now face us can be met. For not only would SP solve the international or global problems it is specifically designed for, it would also have profoundly beneficial effects *within* individual nation states. It would restore genuine democracy and, through its higher global taxes on corporations and markets, also restore well-funded public services and the elimination of poverty in the Third World.

Perhaps one day, were it to succeed in its objective, it is not inconceivable that ISPO might eventually become part of the UN organisation itself (UN-ISPO) constituting the first democratic world parliament. Were the model of civil society being invited to adopt SP to be formalised and used to provide direct, democratic civil society representation at the UN, the necessary justification for nation states to relinquish some of their sovereignty to the UN would then exist. The world parliament UN-ISPO would represent need not necessarily, however, consist of representatives. For with modern technology, it is not inconceivable that many, if not all, people of the world could have an electronic vote and, for those without such technology, other methods could be devised. Additionally, for any proposed measure to qualify for such a global referendum, the test applied would be whether its unilateral implementation would have a positive or negative impact on a nation's competitiveness, capital markets, employment, etc. Only those measures likely to have a *negative* impact would qualify. All other measures could, of course, be dealt with by individual national governments alone. In this way a democratic framework that both obliges and allows member states to implement appropriate policies on a global and simultaneous basis would then be in position. Such a framework therefore encompasses both global unity and national diversity and completely avoids the need for a global super-state. Furthermore, if all states can regulate global competition satisfactorily through UN-ISPO, the need for them to 'gang up' into economic (and ultimately political) units such as the EU, NAFTA, ASEAN, etc. in order to compete more effectively against one another would have become entirely superfluous. And that is to say nothing of the bureaucratic waste and democratic deficit that these super-states invariably entail. Indeed, in contrast to the UN we have today, such a democratic framework of governance through a combination of global referenda and nation states would, for the first time, allow all nations to act simultaneously in unity. Only then could all nations of the world be said to constitute truly 'united nations'. This vision is, perhaps, close to the role the founders of the UN spiritually intended it to fulfil when establishing it from amongst the ashes and global destruction of World War II. I sincerely hope it will not require a third world war before it finally becomes reality.

SP CHANGE MEASURES

As indicated earlier in this book, it may be felt that the 'stabilisation' and 'access' measures alone are insufficient to mobilise sufficient public support and, therefore, at least the first sub-stage of the 'change' measures would have to be clear from the outset. I suggest, however, that a decision on the content of the sub-stages might be left for another day. For to imagine that any group of people, however blessed in intelligence and wisdom, could today set out a full range of measures to solve all world problems would of course be ludicrous. Such is the state of the world, however, that formulating the most obviously urgent measures should not be beyond them. When the time came, the necessary research could be carried out to evaluate the strength of public identification with further reform measures after which a decision could be taken. After all, during the many years it will undoubtedly take to successfully campaign for the adoption of SP, and as our problems will regrettably doubtless worsen and become more obvious during that time, the content of the initial sub-stage(s) could be developed as the campaign progresses. The resulting additional measures could then be added to the already existing ones provided those who have already adopted SP are willing to do so. Indeed, since the nature and severity of world problems is bound to alter over the years of a campaign, it is clear that the whole process of formulating the measures of SP must be flexible and dynamic. Its measures could therefore evolve and emerge in line with public opinion which will, it is to be hoped, itself evolve towards the ecological view. Changing people's minds towards this view would, after all, be the underlying or subconscious message of the campaign.

Alternatively, 'change measures' could be dealt with as a completely separate process that followed global adoption of SP in the form only of its 'stabilisation' and 'access' measures. For if that were achieved and implemented, the institution of democratic global governance that UN-ISPO would represent would then be available as a platform from which 'change measures' could be formulated. Having achieved global adoption once, both governments and peoples could and would then see its value and, it is to be hoped, would then be better able to follow the pattern of global simultaneous implementation again and again with increasing ease as the need arises.

The holistic framework of global simultaneous implementation – a range of policies common to rich and poor countries alike - provides the framework for the change of attitude required to the way we view the basic needs of the poor. As Jeremy Seabrook points out:

"Basic needs cannot easily be defined independently of the particular cultural context in which they are formulated. The values, customs and traditions of any culture will modify these needs in different ways...

Indeed, in Western consumer society, our fundamental needs have become opaque to us, for they are mediated by such a dense forest of objects, artefacts and symbols that we find it hard to distinguish the boundaries where our needs cease and the things which claim to answer them begin. Human need merges imperceptibly with economic necessity: consumer confidence swiftly becomes moral imperative.

It is not difficult to draw up an abstract account of basic needs. And as far as survival goes, such abstractions may be adequate. It is simply that no one lives in such a state of socially and culturally disarmed nakedness. That is why even the most comprehensive programmes that start out from this level remain unsatisfactory...

It is significant that it is only for the poor that programmes are drawn up purporting to answer 'basic needs'. No one ever thinks of offering the rich such a formula. ...

If there is to be any such undertaking, it must be as applicable to high-consuming rich societies as to those eking out an existence on the edge of survival. For it should not be imagined that the lives of the poorest are any less complex than the lives of those who live in a world of industrialised plenty. ...

This is why we are in no position to propose, to the poor of the

Earth, remedies which we conspicuously avoid for ourselves. ...
It is time to call home the experts. It is time to bring back the
professionals, the economists and all those who take their
costly know-how to the Third World to discover answers to
poverties in which we are all implicated. Let them, instead,
discover first how to cure the maladies of wealth. Then we
shall find that the solution to the problem of poverty will take
care of itself.[11]

SP therefore provides the framework within which the
professionals can refashion their ideas in a more appropriate
way which applies both to rich and poor alike.

Perhaps the best guidance we could wish for in founding
the principles upon which 'change measures' should be
designed comes from E.F. Schumacher's "Small is Beautiful".
Such measures might include, for example, a staged reduction
in the maximum permitted size of corporations by embark-
ing on a de-merging programme. A reorientation towards
intermediate technology in both advanced and developing
nations. New patterns of ownership. A fixed ratio of salary
between highest and lowest paid. The reconstruction of rural
community life. The phasing out of violent technologies and
practices in industry and agriculture. An obligation to use
only organic farming methods. A complete reorientation of
education towards wisdom. A complete reorientation of
science and technology to incorporate ethics into their very
structure. Various tax reforms would also be required as part
of a gradual move towards 'eco-taxation'.

SP AND BENEFITS FOR BUSINESS

Planning 'change measures' should involve input from a
variety of people including not only current pioneers such as

---

[11] From *Basic Needs* by Jeremy Seabrook published in Resurgence No. 193,
March/April 1999.

Intermediate Technology Development Group, Scott Bader Commonwealth and the Soil Association but also, most importantly, from business leaders themselves. We have seen above that SP would be low-risk for business, the constraints being placed upon it applying to all businesses simultaneously. From a competitive point of view, shareholders and managers alike would therefore be in no worse a position compared to other companies. After all, a limit on the maximum size of corporations would also introduce an important self-regulating constraint which promotes healthy and fair competition as well as an avoidance of monopolies, cartels and other unwelcome concentrations of power. Such constraints applying only to major corporations rather than to small and medium sized concerns would also represent a positive 'tax on the big' thus promoting and recognising the intrinsic social and economic value of small enterprise.

This general alleviation of intense competitive pressures should come as some welcome relief to business people who are at the 'sharp end' of competition. Whilst some might fear an outflow of investment from major corporations, it should be remembered that all capital markets would be subject to similar restraints and therefore the relative attractiveness of capital markets to investors should remain stable. It should therefore allow businessmen to re-deploy their talents in more creative and imaginative ways that put people before profits and excessive executive salaries thereby benefiting not only their companies but society as a whole. (Not being an economist, however, I must confess that I am unclear as to which measures would be most appropriate.) In the context of an adoption campaign, the support of so-called "ethical investment fund" managers giving priority to companies that had adopted SP would also be beneficial.

One thing business hates is uncertainty. A further benefit for business, therefore, would be that all SP measures are to be implemented and staged in a way that business could plan for constructively. Such changes would doubtless present new challenges and opportunities. During this period of transition, it should also be understood that the "special directors" I propose could act not only in a *restraining* capacity but also in an *advisory* one that could be very positive and valuable. This would include advising their board and staff colleagues on matters such as sustainable development, The Natural Step[12], Employee Share Ownership Schemes (ESOPs), community development within the corporation itself, community development between the corporation and local organisations, and so on. They could also be responsible for implementing them were they to form part of the measures of SP. Keeping company directors and staff in touch with the great benefits their contribution in the form of the Development Tax would bring to the poorest people in non-industrialised countries and promoting direct links between them would also be a very worthwhile function the "special directors" could perform. They would therefore represent active and dynamic sources of both restraint and advice, able to act at the heart of corporate affairs.

Whether the proposed 'corporation tax for equity swap' were included in SP or not, I suggest some leading business people must by now be aware that the behavioural mode of predatory competition in which they are locked as they 'race to the bottom'[13] cannot go on for much longer before a major crisis of some kind occurs. The seeking of ever higher short-term profits and relative safety from unwelcome takeovers through daily mergers and acquisitions is causing havoc with countless lives, to say nothing of the detrimental knock-on effects on the economy and society as a whole:

[12] *The Natural Step* is a scientific process designed for corporations to achieve environmental sustainability.
[13] *When Corporations Rule the World*. David Korten. Pages 229-237. Kumarian Press Inc. and Berrett-Koehler Publishers, 1995.

"**Anger as AXA culls 2,000 jobs after GRE takeover.**
AXA, the insurance giant, provoked a storm of protest yesterday after it announced that it is to cut 2,000 jobs following its £3.45bn takeover of Guardian Royal Exchange. The scale of the cuts, which include 1,500 compulsory redundancies over two years, is significantly higher than was suggested in February when AXA won the auction for GRE. Its success at the time was due in part to the fact that, unlike rival bidder Royal & Sun Alliance, which was talking of 5,000 job cuts, AXA had talked only of modest staff reductions. Mark Wood, chief executive of AXA's UK offshoot Sun Life & Provincial, said in February when the deal was announced that these [redundancies] would be "in the hundreds, not the thousands". ... Yesterday Mr Wood said that, while he was sad for those affected by the cuts, he believed it was better to announce the redundancies as a block to reduce uncertainty."[14]

The untold damage to society caused by this business environment can only ultimately end in disaster. It must surely be in the longer term interests of business and of shareholders for transition to occur in a staged and orderly manner as is proposed under SP. For the alternative is a crisis of proportions that could lead to strife and chaos which cannot be in anyone's interests. As a businessman myself, I would therefore be hopeful that my colleagues leading tomorrow's major corporations might realise before it is too late that, for them too, adopting SP represents their best option for the future. One can only hope they would be willing to play their part.

SP AND BENEFITS FOR POLITICIANS

Crucially, implementation of SP only once all nations have adopted it allows politicians room for radical manoeuvre: it allows them openly to adopt SP risking neither the national interest nor their own personal positions. It allows them to

[14] *The Independent.* 11th May 1999.

go out on a limb in open support of SP without needing to alter their current views or policies which are necessarily determined by, and designed for, the current competitive context. As public support grows, it is to be hoped that politicians, too, will come to see SP as the only way of liberating themselves from the increasing tyranny of 'big end' capitalism in the form of transnational corporations and global financial markets.

When asked, most politicians tell us how they nobly chose their profession to make a "real difference to people's lives". But as the vortex created by the competitive pressures of advanced capitalism exerts itself with ever-greater force upon society, it determines the ever-decreasing parameters within which politicians are left to make the "difference" of which they speak. On the one hand symptoms of social decay caused by unfettered competition multiply all around us necessitating greater public expenditure and more regulation, whilst on the other, global markets effectively veto such measures leaving major corporations to demand free subsidies to deter them from moving production to other countries.

> "Hopes of saving Rover's car factory at Longbridge were dealt a severe blow last night after its German owner, BMW, rejected a British aid package.
> BMW said it did not agree with UK officials on details of the subsidy offer to help build a new medium-sized car at Rover's West Midlands plant. ...
> The Department of Trade and Industry had been expected to offer around £180m in return for more than £1.7bn of investment by BMW... 'They did not think they were in a poker game and that is what caused the surprise,' said one source....
> BMW is now believed to be looking more seriously at siting the plant in Hungary..."[15]

[15] *The Independent.* 20th March 1999.

Such is the vortex that, by now, makes the "difference" of which our politicians like to speak seem rather pathetic indeed. As George Soros concludes:

> "Today the ability of the state to provide for the welfare of its citizens has been severely impaired by the ability of capital to escape taxation and onerous employment conditions by moving elsewhere. … The dismantling of the welfare state is a relatively new phenomenon, and its full effect has not yet been felt."[16]

Apart from the re-regulation of capital markets, SP's ban on political funding by big business (if not all business) would allow politicians to complete their liberation and so to regain their rightful, independent position as guarantors of democratic society accountable to, and only to, the people. Instead of the contempt in which they are now generally held by the public, this would at last earn them the respect they ought normally to deserve.

SP AND BENEFITS FOR THE PUBLIC

The most obvious benefit for the public is that SP offers us all a way out of a situation that is beyond the control of our elected leaders and of business leaders themselves: a situation which must, unless something is done, lead to social collapse and, ultimately, to war.

Beyond this, however, is the benefit of a re-birth of democracy: *quality* democracy in which the people can freely determine how they live without being dictated to by financial markets or by the damaging distortion of corporate intrusion. Such is the insidious nature of these influences that few recognise their very real impact on our lives. As businesses compete ever more fiercely employing labour-saving technologies that cause job security to evaporate, who is prepared

---

[16] *The Crisis of Global Capitalism.* George Soros. Little, Brown & Co, 1998.

to resist employers' demands for longer working hours?[17] But the pressure of longer hours plays a part in causing stress, relationship problems and increased divorce rates. The same insecurity drives us to extreme lengths to push our children to achieve results beyond what would be natural for their age in a quest for their future job security. Schools too are placed under competitive pressure to produce examination passes and, in doing so, perhaps neglect other important educational aspects, becoming less like schools and more like qualification factories. Indeed, countries like Britain or the USA which have fully embraced free-market competition and a highly restricted welfare state are necessarily accompanied by extreme gaps between rich and poor.[18] In a general sense, it could be said that greater competition has engendered a decay in moral values by substituting them with those of the market – a decay in which it should not surprise us if some of our youngsters turn to violence, faced as they are by meaninglessness, hopelessness and alienation.[19]

In spite of all this, we tend simply to say "that's life" or to see these pressures as simply "a sign of the times". But we must realise that it does not *have* to be this way. These acute pressures,

---

[17] "Britons work longer hours and come behind most other northern continental states in wage levels. Britain's poorest 20% receives only 7% of the national income, whereas the richest 20% gets 41%... In Britain, 10% of people are in one parent families, a much higher proportion than in other parts of Europe. More than 50% of single parent households in Britain are classed as below the poverty line, ..." From an EU survey, *The Guardian*, 25th June 1999.

[18] "**Preventable deaths rise as health gap widens**. THE HEALTH gap between rich and poor in Britain is the widest on record and is continuing to grow, researchers report today. Increasing inequality in income, lifestyle, educational opportunities and jobs is resulting in thousands of extra deaths in the most deprived inner cities. ... The most embarrassing finding for ministers is that those suffering the most sickness and the highest death rates are Labour voters. ... The researchers say the gap between rich and poor has widened faster in Britain and that levels of poverty are higher than in much of Europe." *The Independent*, 2nd December 1999.

[19] For example, the bombings perpetrated allegedly by extreme right wing neo-nazi groups of young people against minority groups in London. (April 1999).

though we may not realise it at first, are the direct result of advanced and highly competitive markets. These are the pressures that SP is designed to alleviate. If successful, it would allow us to fashion a *new quality of life* rather than merely a *standard of living*: a simpler but infinitely more fulfilling lifestyle more consistent with Right Livelihood and Right Human Relations. For without SP, society – like politics – can only remain paralysed in a state of pseudo-democracy, destined to further decay and ultimately culminating – sooner or later – in disaster.

And this is to say nothing of the dramatic improvements the implementation of SP would bring to countless millions in poorer countries around the world through its cancellation of Third World Debt and its replacement with freely donated funds in the form of the Tobin and Development taxes levied on financial market transactions and on all major corporations. It would at last permanently break the cycle of debt, population growth, degradation and decay that has been allowed to continue for far too long.

CAMPAIGNING AND SPIRITUAL VALUES

Naturally, the kind of changes proposed can be neither meaningful nor lasting nor valid without a growing realisation amongst all people that "humanity cannot live by bread alone", i.e. that we need to embrace an attitude to life which rejects greed and envy and recognises when enough is enough - and that lives and acts in the secure knowledge of these truths. Indeed, a wholesale rejection of crude materialism and a revival of spiritual values is required. Since adoption of SP requires no change in behaviour, be it of individuals, businesses or governments, it would be facile to think that on the day the last country adopts SP and implementation proceeds, that revival of spiritual values will occur and we are all suddenly going to live in an ecological manner. The gradual process of adoption of SP therefore gives those who have chosen to adopt the time in which to contemplate their ways of life, and their values and to seek to make appropriate changes. Adoption should therefore be seen not only as a *political* choice but as a *life* choice: and with that choice comes a personal obligation to do what we can, in whatever way we can, to improve matters even now, in small ways, at least as importantly as in large. Indeed, whilst it has been stressed that the behaviour of people, organisations or nations *need* not change, it should be clear that adoption of SP should act as a spur to making whatever material changes are possible in our own daily lives and to bringing the need for humanising reforms to the attention of politicians and business leaders around the world. Such action is bound to be different for each of us but for the relatively well off it could include reducing our consumption, buying organic and 'Fair Trade' foods and providing greater support to NGOs and charities. For all of us, engaging in peaceful protest against the WTO or other similar institutions is vital if our current problems are to be brought to public attention. As the numbers adopting SP grow, so that growing community of SP can also help each other in promoting and making those changes.

Just as the public would be encouraged gradually to shift its outlook and life-style towards a more ecological view during the adoption campaign, so businesses who today largely pay only lip service to 'environmentally friendly' products, would have to recognise their customers' tastes were gradually changing towards products built to last rather than built to become obsolete. Indeed, if adoption became so widespread that completion of the process ceased to be a mere possibility and became a probability, businesses would be forced to reorient themselves towards compliance with the measures laid down in SP even before the adoption process had been completed.

Similarly, whilst it accepts governments and nations for what they are and requires no change in their behaviour, the growing numbers of people around the world that adopt SP would serve as an ever louder call to political leaders to heed the need for democracy characterised by truly free and open societies free from corporate or other inappropriate influences. Like businesses, the adoption process as it gathers pace, will require politicians to make what changes they can. They could actively reduce their dependency on corporate funding for example.

The adoption campaign, and in particular the dynamics of the Principle of Openness and Challenge, would therefore serve as a kind of subconscious, spiritual call to all people, organisations and governments of the world to recognise that we need to embrace spiritual values and a life-style more consistent with the needs of human nature and of Nature itself. Whilst the impetus for such spiritual and material reform must come from within, the adoption campaign would at least provide conducive conditions in which it is encouraged to flourish. For in today's society based on consumerism and competition, even those of us who recognise a more ecological life-style to be necessary can safely fail to act on it, secure in the knowledge that our behaviour will go unnoticed and unquestioned. The adoption campaign, once it gains momentum, would therefore help to create the necessary social pressure which discourages such behaviour. For without SP to rally around and focus upon, it is doubtful that vast numbers of people will come to realise and act upon this wisdom on their own. Perhaps most important of all is the call for global co-operation that SP represents itself predicates a spiritual value: the spiritual value of co-operation and community.

In seeking to do what each of us can, in *Small is Beautiful*, Schumacher concludes:

"Everywhere people ask: 'What can I actually do?' The answer is simple as it is disconcerting: we can, each of us, work to put our own inner house in order. The guidance we need for this work cannot be found in science or technology, the value of which utterly depends on the ends they serve; but it can still be found in the traditional wisdom of mankind."

Important contributions to helping us put our "inner houses" in order are thankfully freely available. One such contribution is M. Scott Peck's *The Road Less Traveled*, but as Schumacher suggests, there are others. What is clear is that the current widespread absence of spiritual values in society is a crucial factor in causing the problems we now face. This absence might itself be reason enough to embark on the enterprise that SP represents for the decay of such values is doubtless due in large part to competition itself. Indeed, it could be said that ethics and morality are the first casualties of competition because competition is a mode of behaviour in which self-survival necessarily takes precedence over tolerance, compassion or fairness. It therefore leaves no room for higher values, least of all those advocated by the traditional religions. Most leading clergy, particularly Christian, would, I think, agree that the lack of appeal of the church to the majority represents another casualty of our current way of life.[20] It should, therefore, cause them to take a more active and robust stance in confronting the problems we face. Against this background, perhaps some churchmen and churchwomen would do well to heed the words of Alice Bailey:

"Churchmen need to remember that the human spirit is greater than the churches and greater than their teaching. In the long run, that human spirit will defeat them and proceed triumphantly into the kingdom of God, leaving them far behind unless they enter as an humble part of the mass of men.

[20] *See The Guardian*. 13th November 1999: "Number in Church on Sundays dips below 1m."

... Nothing under heaven can arrest the progress of the human soul on its long pilgrimage from darkness to light, from the unreal to the real, from death to immortality and from ignorance to wisdom. If the great organised religious groups of churches in every land and composing all faiths do not offer spiritual guidance and help, humanity will find another way."[21]

The adoption campaign - or the 'march through emptiness' – as it gathers pace and numbers will, I hope, become an increasingly powerful spiritual experience. As the growing chorus of increasing numbers becomes ever louder and political parties and governments around the world, one by one, gradually succumb to adoption, there can be few other processes imaginable likely to demonstrate the power and triumph of the human spirit. As a world-wide process it would show us all – rich and poor, black and white, Christian and Muslim that we are all one: all one in our imperfection, all one in the brotherhood of humanity and all one in the eye of our respective God. It should, therefore, provide a useful spur to all of us to take the time to rediscover that essential traditional wisdom of mankind. In this spirit, I respectfully suggest that churches of all religious persuasions could also set an example by adopting SP.

CAMPAIGNING METHODS AND STRATEGY

Let us now briefly imagine a world strategy for our 'march through emptiness': a strategy for the adoption campaign. Perhaps the first task would be to gain a public profile for the concept of SP itself. An appropriate forum might be the various Earth Summit meetings or the World Social Forum through the help, not only of ISPO itself, but of supportive non-governmental organisations. Following this, perhaps the non-industrialised countries representing the poorest people

[21] *Problems of Humanity*. Alice A. Bailey. Lucis Publishing, 1964.

of the world would be the best and most fitting place to commence the adoption process. As has been pointed out, these nations have nothing to lose by adoption and everything to gain.

If a wide media profile had been achieved at such meetings along with adoption by the world's poorest countries, let us imagine what the new situation might be like. Instead of the usual agreements concerning targets for reduced emissions, (which everybody knows will never be achieved), the public statements coming out from Earth Summits will be quite different. They will say that non-industrialised and developing nations are no longer interested in fantasy targets for treating symptoms - they are interested in *practical action to treat the root cause!* In adopting SP, the bulk of non-industrialised and developing nations would then be seen to *set the example* as well as an open challenge to their more developed and advanced counterparts. Thereafter, the focus of publicity and international public pressure for adoption would then be placed fairly and squarely on the industrialised and more developed countries. Whilst this is being attended to, national SP organisations would have prepared detailed strategies and priorities for targeting political parties in Western pseudo-democracies. Adoption by a large number of non-industrialised and some developing countries having been achieved, the stage for the battle of hearts and minds in Western countries would have been well set.

One weapon that might be used in this battle, harnessing the non-party-political character of SP also outlined earlier, is the power of music. This might sound bizarre but no doubt many of us can remember the Band Aid/Live Aid concerts which had an enormous international impact. Although short-lived, their contribution was more than simply a gesture of aid. It was action that transcended government: action which *set an example* to governments.

Leading musicians have enormous responsibility and potential in terms of their considerable influence, particularly on the younger generation. They would have enormous power, if channelled correctly, to spur the process of adoption as well as promoting a feeling of world community.[22] After all, like so many popular songs, SP is fundamentally about peace, reconciliation and winning through against heavy odds in a good cause.

Music, along with art and other manifestations of culture, are perhaps the only things that make sense to us in a crazy world where traditional religion regrettably seems to have lost its relevance to so many. Appreciation of rock music now spans two generations or more – that is a lot of voters. With a suitable coordinator to mobilise musicians and others in support of SP, more or less regular concerts or other events are envisaged to raise funds both for whatever latest human disaster comes across our TV screens and for ISPO. This will provide funds for a campaign as well as for the victims of the disaster concerned, whilst having an enormous impact on the adoption campaign itself.

The linking of the SP adoption campaign to the plight and suffering caused by natural and other disasters is entirely appropriate. There is increasing recognition that the causes of many such disasters can be traced back to man's inappropriate use of land through, for example, over-intensive farming that can cause soil erosion leading to mud-slides, etc.:

> "**World is facing plague of disasters.** …The combination of growing climatic instability, due to global warming, with the concentration of the world's poor in ever more vulnerable places, will set off 'chain reactions of devastation', the Red Cross says, in its World Disasters Report for 1999. …

---

[22] Many of us can also perhaps remember Bob Geldof's astonishing and impromptu TV encounter with Mrs. Thatcher on the subject of foreign aid where he, unlike just about anyone else in the world at that time, clearly got the upper hand.

The Red Cross study highlights two environmental problems which are already making natural catastrophies much worse – global warming and the mass felling of forests. Climatic warming…is tending to make extreme weather events, such as hurricanes or droughts, even more intense, and is leading to rising sea levels all round the world. Deforestation is removing the natural protection that vegetation gives the earth's surface and leading to landslides and much more severe flooding. When these are combined with socio-economic trends, such as the movement of millions of people to the unplanned mega-cities of the developing world, often on vulnerable coastlines, the effect is explosive."[23]

Practices such as deforestation are encouraged by the increasing burden of foreign debt as well as by the imposition of Structural Adjustment Programmes both of which exert extreme pressure on poorer nations. Global warming too is a symptom of the resource abuse that characterises our unsustainable way of life. As we wake up to the inter-connectedness of man and the environment so we see such disasters are often caused or exacerbated by global competition: the root cause of our two world problems. In attempting to solve them the power of music can and will make an enormous difference. After all, global capital may know no national borders, but neither does music.

If adoption by mainstream parties in the majority of advanced and more-developed countries as well as by most non-industrialised countries were achieved, that would leave a rump of countries outstanding. Many such countries are probably non-democratic with their governments supported in power only by western national (or corporate) interests. The force of public opinion from both advanced and non-industrial nations as expressed through their adoption of SP, combined with the possible (but last resort) use of consumer

---

[23] *The Independent*, 24th June 1999.

boycotts, would then put considerable pressure on those western governments or corporations concerned to reverse their policies towards these countries and instead encourage their adoption.

Reverting to the idea of Schumacher Eggs, it is also envisaged that whilst individual members of the public could display their adoption of SP by means of a badge or car window sticker, environmental groups, charities, schools or businesses that become members of ISPO by adopting SP could also do so by displaying their bronze or silver eggs on their web-sites, letterheads or other literature. All this kind of publicity - akin to the "Intel Inside"[24] effect – will also be very valuable. The increasing number of organisations of all types doing so will provide daily encouragement to us all whilst serving as a challenge to all those who have not yet adopted. Above all, perhaps, it will show that we are no longer ashamed openly to admit our world problems and our open determination to address them.

---

[24] "*Intel-Inside*" is a registered trademark of Intel Corp.

9. Symptoms, Causes and Non-governmental Organisations

"Everything in this world has to have a *structure*, otherwise it is chaos."[1]

Returning to today's world, let us look at the symptoms and causes of our two world problems as they relate to the activities of charities and other non-governmental organisations (NGOs) and as seen in the light of the solution SP provides.

SYMPTOMS AND CAUSES

There appears to be growing recognition of the causal links between the concerns of various NGOs and the importance of this in demonstrating to politicians the wider effects of policy and more comprehensive ways of formulating new policy. One welcome example is "The Real World Coalition" which consists of NGOs including Christian Aid, Employment Policy Institute, Friends of the Earth, Transport 2000, WWF, Population Concern and many others brought together by the central body, Forum for the Future. The idea, for example, is that unemployment (represented by one NGO) causes poverty (represented by another NGO). Poverty in turn causes ill-health (represented by yet a further NGO) and so on. These causal links rightly suggest that coordinated action is called for.

We should nevertheless remember that all these, and the many other problems and concerns of NGOs, represent

[1] *Small is Beautiful.* E.F. Schumacher. Abacus, 1974.

merely *symptoms*. For unless one can trace these causal links, one by one, back to a *root cause*, all these NGOs surely represent just linked sets of symptoms floating free of the root cause, which in the meantime, remains unaddressed and free to worsen. This in turn allows existing symptoms to intensify thus causing new sets of symptoms to arise – 'symptoms of symptoms', if you will, or a continuation of yet further causal links. As a response to this, yet more NGOs will doubtless be created to cope, thus diluting financial and other resources still further.

As an 'Insider's Guide', we should all be agreed that the root cause of these problems is destructive global competition and its accompanying decay in spiritual values. Without an organisation focused upon achieving a political and spiritual shift of emphasis, therefore, the root cause can only continue to remain largely unaddressed and symptoms can consequently only worsen. An organisation focused solely on openly, honestly and directly addressing the root cause by carrying on a vigorous, unashamed and unequivocal political and spiritual campaign for an ecological, (rather than environmental), approach to reforming the capitalist system is therefore urgently needed. That organisation is ISPO.

As support for ISPO gathers force it will create an entirely new situation and let us consider what it might be like. With the existence of ISPO, each NGO can be secure in the knowledge that ISPO is focused solely on attacking the root cause of the problem whilst they attend to their particular branches of it. The concerns and efforts of all NGOs can therefore begin to sit in a proper relationship not only to each other, but to the root cause itself. Each NGO should thereby be better able to see the relevance of its own sphere of activity as vitally necessary but, nevertheless, as secondary to the primary objective of treating the root cause. This, I suggest, at last brings structure and clarity to the whole problem.

Furthermore, the ability of all to better identify their proper place in the scheme of things therefore permits those working broadly in the same fields to combine more readily their efforts with all the positive knock-on effects that this would have in terms of concentrating both effort and finance.

Without widespread support for ISPO, the unintended confusion or "free-floating symptoms effect" remains highly dangerous because it allows those that exacerbate the problems NGOs are trying to solve to carry on doing so. For as symptoms become ever more endemic and complex, who is to say which came first or which is more urgent than another? The clear distinction and relationship between symptoms and root cause therefore enables the proper communication of the various concerns of NGOs not least to the general public who, in the end, must be mobilised to exert pressure on politicians for reform.

ENVIRONMENTALISM OR ECOLOGISM?

Another confusing aspect of the world of NGOs appears to be the difference in their approaches to treating the root cause of the problem (if they seek to treat it at all). This is damaging because it causes further confusion in the mind of the public. Some NGOs seem to feel that the environmental approach of seeking to 'manage' capitalism is all that is required as opposed to the more radical approach advocated by ecologists. *Environmentalists* and *ecologists* are effectively divided (according to Dobson, 1990 p13.) as follows. Ecologists or ecologism

> "argues that care for the environment presupposes radical change in our relationship with it, and thus in our mode of social and political life"

whereas environmentalists,

"would argue for a 'managerial' approach to environmental problems, secure in the belief that they can be solved without fundamental changes in present values or patterns of production and consumption."[2]

Whether one has sympathy for one or other, let's look at our options. If we take the environmental (rather than ecological) approach, we must have absolute faith in a technological fix becoming available before it is too late. This is because the environmentalist approach allows the root cause of our problems to continue to grow essentially unchecked. This means a continued commitment to growth in a finite environment which, in turn, must mean that they ultimately believe that a massive technological fix can and will provide a way to square the circle. Technology, if anything, has served to intensify social and environmental problems rather than to solve them. As Martell points out:

"In short, technical solutions fail either because they sustain growth to overshoot in other areas or because they are ineffective in holding back growth where they are supposed to. In both cases the problem proves to be continuing growth in a finite system. Technical solutions which attempt to sustain growth or vainly try to curb it are inadequate to the resolution of problems of resource availability, pollution, food production, population and industrial output because they do not deal with the root problem, which is growth itself in a system in which there are natural limits."[3]

Common sense would lead us to conclude, therefore, that unless we care nothing for our children and future generations we have no alternative but to follow the ecological approach and to follow it quickly. One would also think that environmentalists (as defined above), being similarly concerned would surely see this also. Even were it theoretically

[2] *Green Political Thought: An Introduction.* Dobson. Unwin Hyman, London 1990.
[3] *Ecology & Society.* Martell. Polity Press, 1994.

possible for a technological fix to be developed, how likely is it that it will arrive in time? How can we know it will really work? What fall-back position is there if it doesn't?

A further possibility is that they believe that the direction of capitalism can be altered simply by 'managing' it perhaps because they see no viable way of achieving more radical results. In this case, they either delude themselves in settling for a 'solution' which is, in fact, no solution at all. Or perhaps they genuinely believe they can successfully 'manage' capitalism towards sustainability in which case they cannot properly understand its nature nor the competitive context in which businessmen operate. As George Soros points out with reference to both environmental and social problems:

> "...it can be anticipated that the world economy will be dominated even more than it is today by publicly owned international corporations. Severe competition will not allow them to pay much heed to social concerns. They will, of course, pay lip service to worthy causes such as the environment, particularly if they have direct dealings with the general public, but they will not be able to afford to maintain employment to the detriment of profits."[4]

Or David Korten:

> "We hear repeatedly from defenders of corporate libertarianism that the greening of management within a globalized free market will provide the answer to the world's social and environmental problems. With financial markets demanding maximum short-term gains and corporate raiders standing by to trash any company that isn't externalizing every possible cost, efforts to fix the problem by raising the social consciousness of managers misdefine the problem. There are plenty of socially conscious managers. The problem is a predatory system that makes it difficult for them to survive. This

---

[4] *The Crisis of Global Capitalism.* George Soros. Little, Brown & Co, 1998.

creates a terrible dilemma for managers with a true social vision of the corporation's role in society. They must either compromise their vision or run a great risk of being expelled by the system."[5]

Locked into competition as they are, therefore, even the world's leading business people are as powerless to control the capitalist system as anyone else. So why environmentalists or those taking a similar managerial approach think they can control what businessmen manifestly cannot is bewildering. Enlightenment can only come from informing themselves from the abundant literature available.

Similarly, whilst I am far from condoning the harmful activities of certain multi- or transnational corporations and vigorously support all efforts to deter them from those activities, surely the Green movement achieves little by demonising these companies and their executives. They exist and must survive in a highly competitive environment driven by the ever-higher demands for short-term profits and the fear of unwelcome takeovers. In such an environment it should not be difficult to see why their guiding credo is: "If we don't do it, our competitors will" – and they are right. So let us stop demonising them. They are as much subject to, and unable to control, the highly competitive pressures that characterise the environment in which they must operate as anyone else. In understanding that what we are dealing with is a *systemic* problem, we must surely recognise that it is the *root cause* that must demand the urgent attention of NGOs and others.

NGOs taking a 'managerial' approach should also consider what might happen if their strategy were to prove unsuccessful. Having committed themselves to 'managing' capitalism, what happens if in the end they fail to do so adequately? What would happen if all their targets for achieving 'sustainability' are

[5] *When Corporations Rule the World*. David Korten. Kumarian Press Inc. and Berrett-Koehler Publishers, 1995.

missed (as indeed most, if not all, have been so far) and they in fact fail adequately to manage capitalism? By the time that failure became clear, it would already be too late. The same would apply to those who advocate the de-linking of communities from the global economy by creating their own self-reliant economies. Welcome and valid though such efforts are, they fail to offer a feasible alternative to the mass of people living in urban areas who, like it or not, are bound to remain largely dependent upon the mainstream economy. If and when social or economic collapse occurs, even small scale community initiatives are unlikely to escape the ensuing chaos.

Furthermore, today's activists, single-issue pressure groups, NGOs, trade unions and others who have traditionally focused their campaigns on forcing national legislative change through direct action, media coverage, lobbying, etc. must urgently wake up and see that these approaches alone are substantially out-dated and no longer very effective. For the competitive global market has severely curtailed the ability of governments to respond in any meaningful way to those demands. Successive waves of trade rules, de-regulation, privatisation and competitive tax cutting are all functions of a competitive global market over which politicians no longer have any substantial control. What, therefore, is the use of applying pressure on them when the demands of international competitiveness and the dictates of the money markets mean they have few, if any, options open to them? That is not to say that those campaigns are invalid or should be abandoned, but surely they must now become secondary to the primary demand of changing the global system which today constitutes a comprehensive road-block to the achievement of their aims.

Be they NGOs taking a 'managerial' approach or small-scale initiatives seeking independence from the global economy, or be they other campaigns seeking social justice, surely common sense should now tell them to "back both horses". This they can do by continuing their very valid activities as they are now but, at the same time, by adopting SP which is focused on creating systemic change at the global level. For it is this two-pronged approach which is absolutely vital and the key to ultimate success in achieving our common objective of a better world. Were NGOs and others simply to adopt SP and to throw their entire campaigning weight behind it but, in doing so, abandoned their existing campaigns, that would be wholly inadequate. For we need campaigning action *today* if the public is to learn the reality of the abuse and injustice going on in the world. Equally, focusing solely on their existing campaigns without attending to the necessary systemic change their adoption and support of SP would help bring about would also likewise be wholly inadequate. Indeed, we must therefore *do both*, be we individuals, pressure groups, activists, unions or NGOs. After all, the two approaches are entirely compatible: SP in any case only encompasses policies pertaining to the global or international level. Furthermore, adopting SP involves NGOs or others in no significant expense in terms of time or effort. It essentially only requires confirmation of their adoption and, in the case of organisations, the alteration of their web-sites, letterheads and literature to include their bronze Schumacher Egg. In this simple but effective way, therefore, they can 'back both horses' in helping to solve world problems. Indeed, "*act globally, not just locally*" should be our new watchword, for surely, does not the strangle-hold of global markets, corporations and destructive competition now demand that we do both?

PRICING THE ENVIRONMENT

At this point it may be appropriate to mention that there are those who believe capitalism can be successfully brought into harmony with a healthy natural environment through environmental accounting and resource pricing measures. Whilst not wishing to dismiss such approaches altogether, for as Jeff Gates points out, "what gets measured gets managed"[6], I believe Fritz Schumacher should be allowed a final word:

> "To press non-economic values into the framework of the economic calculus, economists use the method of cost/benefit analysis. This is generally thought to be an enlightened and progressive development, as it is at least an attempt to take account of costs and benefits which might otherwise be disregarded altogether. In fact, however, it is a procedure by which the higher is reduced to the level of the lower and the priceless is given a price. It can therefore never serve to clarify the situation and lead to an enlightened decision. All it can do is lead to self-deception or the deception of others; for to undertake to measure the immeasurable is absurd and constitutes but an elaborate method of moving from preconceived notions to foregone conclusions; all one has to do to obtain the desired results is to impute suitable values to the immeasurable costs and benefits. The logical absurdity, however, is not the greatest fault of the undertaking: what is worse, and destructive of civilisation, is the pretence that everything has a price or, in other words, that money is the highest of all values."[7]

CHARITABLE STATUS

Certainly ISPO itself cannot consider adopting charitable status because that status severely inhibits just the kind of overt political approach it is designed to take. Charitable status effectively ensures that, in the political battles that must be fought if beneficial reform is to occur, any organisation having that status has one arm tied behind its back. To the extent that NGOs seek to band together around a central

---

[6] *The Ownership Solution.* Jeff Gates. Penguin, 1998.
[7] *Small is Beautiful.* E.F. Schumacher. Abacus, 1974. Pages 37-38.

body or organisation in order to obtain more combined political clout, it follows that the central body, if it enjoys charitable status, renders itself incapable of the kind of overt political action that is surely required.

NGOs or others that have charitable status can at least *support* the Simultaneous Policy even if that status prevents them from actually *adopting* it. After all, NGOs already have large numbers of good-hearted and loyal supporters who know decisive political action is needed and are fed-up with the current stagnation in political life. NGOs who assist ISPO by encouraging their members to adopt SP can therefore facilitate the political approach outlined in this book, at last allowing their many members to support a world-wide movement for reform. Their members are the ones who, already today, recognise that urgent political action is needed if only the right method for exercising it could be found. In recognising SP as the appropriate method, NGOs and their millions of supporters can thus set the adoption campaign off to a dramatic and flying start, setting an immediate example and challenge to the wider public around the world. Indeed, they would be the first to show the power of unity and co-operation. For if NGOs and others working for social change whose mission and vocation it is to solve world problems cannot co-operate with one another, surely no one else can be expected to set an example. NGOs and all these groups should therefore take up the challenge: in adopting (or at least supporting) SP, they should be the ones to start the 'march through emptiness' and lead it on its road towards World Community.

10. The Call to Commitment

"On the one side, I see the people who think they can cope with our ... crisis by the methods current, only more so; I call them the people of the forward stampede. On the other side, there are people in search of a new life-style, who seek to return to basic truths about man and his world; I call them home-comers. ... In one way or another everybody will have to take sides in this great conflict."[1]

The evidence of the ever-widening gap between rich and poor, between advanced and non-industrial countries, between the healthy environment we would wish to see and the one we currently have all serve to demonstrate that all is not well with our capitalist system. The fall of communism, as embodied by the Soviet command economy, as well as the diminished threat of nuclear war, have revealed capitalism in all its myriad forms to be the world's dominant mode of production. Having achieved supremacy, the need now is for capitalism to examine itself and to put its own house in order. No longer having the luxury of comparing itself to a clearly less attractive alternative, capitalism is now faced with the urgent task of identifying why it is simply failing to work either for the vast majority of humanity or for the natural environment. We must urgently ask ourselves why, by 1992, 20 percent of the world's people who live in the world's wealthiest countries received 82.7 percent of the world's income; why the number of world refugees has increased

[1] *Small is Beautiful.* E.F. Schumacher. Abacus, 1974.

from about 2 million in 1961 to more than 25 million by 1996; why children are living in sewers beneath the streets of some of the world's great cities; why unemployment in advanced countries refuses to go away; why the global environment continues to be degraded and plundered of its natural resources?

The central argument of this book is that both global free financial markets and the fierce competition they engender exert a strangle-hold over national - and therefore international – politics by forcing adherence to macro-economic policies that further encourage social and environmental decay. Whilst our world is rapidly approaching ecological, social or economic disaster it is therefore locked in to politics capable only of marginal and incremental change. The global economic train is, as it were, advancing towards a precipice with brakes which no longer function properly. Since the engine driving it – the competitive capitalist system – is beyond the control even of business leaders there is, I believe, no way to avoid the approaching precipice apart from the Simultaneous Policy or something very similar. Of course the prospect of achieving world-wide adoption seems highly remote – *but what choice do we have?* On the other hand, what do we have to lose by pursuing SP? Indeed, we surely have a great deal to gain: more than merely saving our skins. For we have an opportunity to take the stage of World Community – and thus humanity – to a new spiritual height. Be that as it may, as social decay worsens, surely we must at least attempt to offer people an alternative political choice to the new far-right. Our failure to do so is an open invitation to fascism and likely to have consequences of a kind already seen not so long ago.

As the pace of technological change leaves increasing numbers without meaningful (or any) employment and the disturbing popularity of these 'New Right' political groups

concomitantly gathers force, American economist Ethan
Kapstein, also director of the Council on Foreign Relations,
asks:

> "The world may be moving inexorably towards one of those
> tragic moments that will lead future historians to ask, why was
> nothing done in time? Were the economic and policy elites
> unaware of the profound disruption that economic and tech-
> nological change were causing working men and women?
> What prevented them from taking the steps necessary to
> prevent a global social crisis?"[2]

Given the predicament we now find ourselves in and the
current political geography of the world neither the over-
throw of national governments in favour of a benevolent
global state on the one hand, nor a reversion to small-scale
opting out on the other, seem to represent viable solutions.

David Korten says:

> "The democratic legitimacy of the institutions to which we
> yield power derives from (1) being duly constituted by and
> accountable to the sovereign people, (2) conducting their
> operations according to an appropriate code of morals and
> ethics, and (3) producing desirable consequences for the
> whole. Most are failing on all three counts, not because the
> individuals who head them are corrupt, but because these
> institutions have become too big, too distant, and too captive
> to special interests. Capturing state power, whether by election
> or revolution, does not change this. Nor do reforms that
> simply chip away at the edges of the current structure. This is
> why elections have become meaningless."[3]

But abandoning democratic processes altogether would be
to abandon the only hope of resolving our society's problems,
be it locally, nationally or globally. Instead what we need is to

---

[2] Quoted from *The Global Trap*. Martin & Schumann. Zed Books, 1997.
[3] *When Corporations Rule the World*. David Korten. Kumarian Press Inc. and
Berrett-Koehler Publishers, 1995.

learn to use (pseudo-)democratic processes in the appropriate way. Furthermore, we have surely learnt that only decisive and unified action that goes to the heart of the problem can save us from approaching disaster. Effective solutions are available but they require global co-operation if they are ever to be implemented. In fostering a climate of competition amongst nations, global free capital flows serve only to widen further the gulf that must be bridged if we are to move from a context of competition to one of co-operation; from one of Chaos to one of Community. The tragedy of competition is that it produces a mind-set of mistrust and fear and a narrow mode of behaviour focused solely on self-survival. In a single-minded effort to compete and thus survive, that mind-set not only deters communication and any sense of spiritual values, it also renders us incapable of solving even the most simple of life's problems. Even as world consciousness beckons us to the truths of reconciliation, co-operation and community, the mind-set of competition conspires to obscure them. In our frustration, we instinctively know things are wrong but somehow find it difficult to lay our fingers on what is right:

> "If it can be said that man collectively shrinks back more and more from the Truth, it can also be said that on all sides the Truth is closing in more and more upon man. It might almost be said that, in order to receive a touch of It, which in the past required a lifetime of effort, all that is asked of him now is not to shrink back. And yet how difficult that is!"[4]

What is proposed in this paper represents an attempt to make reaching that Truth a little easier. The Simultaneous Policy offers us a method through which we can, if we so choose, all reach out and touch It. But adopting SP and so joining the 'march through emptiness' towards adoption by all nations - the stage of World Community - will require not

---

[4] *Ancient Beliefs and Modern Superstitions.* Martin Lings. Perennial Books, London, 1964. Quoted from *Small is Beautiful.*

only our readiness to avoid the endless and futile conundrum of whether SP might or might not eventually be achievable but also our unswerving commitment. As M. Scott Peck advises those who attend his community-building work-shops:

> "There is only one major rule. You can't drop out. I have no guns, whips, chains or shackles to enforce this commitment but each one of us is responsible for the success of this group. If you are unhappy with the way things are going – and you will be – it is your responsibility to speak up and voice your dissatisfaction rather than simply pick up your marbles and quietly leave. The expectation is that we will hang in together through periods of doubt, anxiety, anger, depression, and even despair."[5]

And so this book concludes with a call to commitment. Each one of us is responsible for the success of this world: its happiness, its contentment and its peace. Each one of us is called through world consciousness to make a commitment to bringing about a better world through the common support of a world policy based on the new politics of co-operation, Community, Right Livelihood and Right Human Relations.

Some have defined the much-used word "globalisation" as nothing less than "the end of history"[6] and many more have put forward myriad other definitions. Whatever the proper definition might be, surely what matters is that it now demands of humanity what is perhaps our greatest ever challenge. For humanity has reached a point where the limits of our planet force us to find a way of reconciling our own needs not only with what the planet can sustainably and fairly provide for all its inhabitants today, but also with its capacity to provide comfortably for future generations. Today those

---

[5] *The Different Drum.* M. Scott Peck. Arrow, 1987.

[6] *The End of History and the Last Man.* Francis Fukuyama. Avon Books, 1992. It may be worth reflecting that if globalisation continues unchecked, Mr. Fukuyama's definition may prove prophetically apocalyptic.

'future generations' may seem too far removed to represent much more than mere abstraction to us. But as time to meet the challenge becomes ever shorter, the day is fast approaching when, if nothing is done, what today are future generations with whom we feel no real empathy will soon become our very own children and grandchildren into whose eyes we must look to explain why we made no attempt to meet it.

In devising an appropriate politics capable of meeting that challenge, Wolfgang Sachs sums up what its principal features should be; features which the Simultaneous Policy provides, if not surpasses:

"Three ideals emerge for conceiving a politics that could shoulder the responsibility of acting for a diverse but coherent world – regeneration, unilateral self-restraint and the dialogue of civilizations. Regeneration takes into account the fact that the royal road of development has vanished, since there is no longer any ideal of progress to indicate a common direction. Regeneration calls instead for actualizing the particular image of a good society which is present in each culture. As for unilateral self-restraint, this can take the place of the ideal of inter-dependent growth. It implies instead that each country puts its own house in order in such a way that no economic or environmental burden is pushed onto others that would constrain them in choosing their own path. And, finally, a dialogue of civilizations is imperative as the search for peaceful and sustainable coexistence puts the challenge of self-examination before each culture. A simultaneous process of confrontation and synthesis can lead to coherence, while avoiding the pitfalls of homogeneity."[7]

In our modern world, surely these three ideals can only be realised through the medium of widespread if not global consensus: a state of mature international community in which we unite both to conserve our planet and, at the same

---

[7] *Planet Dialectics. Explorations in Environment & Development.* Wolfgang Sachs. Zed Books, 1999.

time, to celebrate and promote the diversity of our nations and cultures. For consensus and co-operation are the active expressions of Community and "The spirit of true community is the spirit of peace."[8]

Many have theorised in terms of 'game theory' about the predicament in which mankind now finds itself. Our current situation is likened to "The Prisoner's Dilemma"[9]. This a game where two men suspected of committing a serious crime are apprehended committing a less serious one. The police have no conclusive proof of their guilt in the more serious crime, and so want them to provide it by each implicating the other. They are interviewed separately, and the police do not allow them to meet or confer. The atmosphere of fear and mistrust is evident. The *game* we should be playing is derived from the children's game, "Chicken", in which each player gets a greater benefit from co-operating than not.[10] Perhaps, therefore, we can learn something from our children in this respect. I suggest the openness and challenge that those adopting the Simultaneous Policy would pose to others offers us just such an opportunity.

In *Global Mind Change*, the late Willis Harman says:

> "One's initial reaction to the idea of imagining a peaceful world is likely to be that it sounds like a simplistic version of 'the power of positive thinking.' It may seem difficult at first to convince oneself that by such an affirmation one is actually doing anything. True, it may be simplistic to believe that if we all just love one another and speak peace, peace will come into the world. It may be simplistic because powerful unconscious forces make our love ambivalent, and our peace tinged with hidden conflict.

[8] *The Different Drum.* M. Scott Peck. Arrow, 1987.

[9] *The Possibility of Cooperation.* M. Taylor. Cambridge University Press, 1988.

[10] "Chicken" is *not* the same as the game known in the USA and Canada which involves daring one another to carry out some potentially dangerous act.

Despite such justifiable caution, it remains the case that a collective belief in the achievability of global peace will contribute toward realizing that goal, just as the collective disbelief is now thwarting it. However, for affirmation to work well we need to be as specific as possible. The affirmation of sustainable peace will be most effective if it is not simply a general 'pray for peace' outlook, but rather affirmation of a fairly specific plausible scenario based on an informed view of the factors and forces involved."[11]

The initiative the creation of ISPO represents and the leadership it offers in promoting the world-wide adoption of SP provides, I suggest, that "fairly specific plausible scenario".

SP has considerable draw-backs to be sure, but it also has many merits. One is the way it restricts itself to policies pertaining to matters which transcend all others: to the natural environment, without which nothing can exist, to the global economy and to world society. It therefore rises above nations, party politics and the politics of individuals. Another is its acceptance of existing nation states, political parties, businesses and individuals for what they are without judgement. Naturally it is to be hoped all states and peoples will embrace true democratic and social principles for, as I have pointed out, even the leading democracies of the so called 'free world' are found seriously wanting. The non-party-political character of SP is also non-confrontational. Inherent in this is the recognition that no one is really to blame for our current predicament. Perhaps its most important merit, however, is the unique feature of revealing anew the hitherto obscured power of co-operation and Community in a way that allows future policy to be separated from the dilemmas and complexities of current policy. In so doing, it makes it easy to support. Once it starts, therefore, it might catch on quicker than we expect.

---

[11] *Global Mind Change*. Willis Harman. Berrett-Koehler Publishers Inc. & Institute of Noetic Sciences, 1998. Page 184.

In transforming global society and economy such that they become more consistent with Nature and the needs of human nature, I should finally add that the Simultaneous Policy also has one other special and over-riding merit. This is its capability, through its widespread adoption campaign, to involve *all* of mankind in a spirit of World Community and common purpose. After all, the path to Ecological Revolution is about more than just the Earth; it is about Humanity. It's about more than just Right Livelihood; it is also about *Right Human Relations*. It is surely in that spirit of global common purpose, co-operation and community that each of us can, *and should*, make this vital transition "from darkness to light, from the unreal to the real, from death to immortality and from ignorance to wisdom".[12]

END

---

[12] *Problems of Humanity*. Alice A. Bailey. Lucis Publishing Co, 1947.

Postscript

The idea of SP was first aired in a letter to Mr Satish Kumar at "Resurgence" in November 1998 and has evolved gradually over the course of many months. During that time, various pre-publication versions have been circulated to a number of eminent ecologists, counter-economists and others. Although there has been much encouraging praise, it is also certainly necessary to consider their criticisms. Before doing so, however, I feel obliged to make a point of self-criticism.

I am keenly aware that, at least at the time of writing, my life-style is very much at odds with what I have written regarding the need to liberate oneself from the masters of greed and envy and to recognise that 'humanity cannot live by bread alone'. My family and I live in a very large house, enjoy holidays abroad, have three children attending private school and so on. Yet in those circumstances the idea for SP came to me in a split second and, therefore, completely by surprise. Since I sincerely believe and stand by what I have written, my current lifestyle leaves me in something of an embarrassing situation and wide open to charges of hypocrisy. I can only say that my dilemma is, I suppose, one that so many of us share to a greater or lesser extent. What must be our common struggle along the road of transformation will therefore be one shared by me in the recognition that I have further to travel than most.

As far as criticism offered by others is concerned, the main one is that, in assuming the individual policies that would make up SP can and will be arrived at, I am presuming a universal vantage point of rationality: a presumption that one can define reforms that can both be successfully applied world-wide and also be beneficial to everybody. Indeed, it is suggested by some critics that such a 'vantage point' or global 'solution' probably cannot exist at all. Instead they argue that human nature and experience suggest that reform is more likely to arise through myriad smaller-scale initiatives of various kinds occurring all over the world. Initially such initiatives will be seen, as many of them are today, as unorthodox but over time they will gradually be adopted, they say, as mainstream practice. Leading on from this is their criticism that the SP approach is too "top-down" and authoritarian. In addition, it has also been asserted that even if support for the concept of SP were to become widespread, the differences of opinion and of priorities among supporters over what specific measures would be appropriate would, they say, make it impossible to come to any kind of final agreement. A further criticism concerns the implementation of existing environmental and other policies. It is feared that nations might use SP as an excuse to delay the implementation of those policies until adoption by all countries had been achieved.

I certainly understand these criticisms and, to some extent, accept them and have amended more recent versions of this paper to answer them. There are, however, some points I would like to make:

Taking the last of these criticisms first, I cannot really see that SP will be used as an excuse for delay. Every policy needs to be tested using the criteria of whether its unilateral implementation would have a *negative* or *positive* impact on national competitiveness. If it is *negative*, then that policy is never going to get implemented without global agreement in any case and should therefore be included in SP. Governments pondering policies that are *positive*, on the other hand, will surely want to implement them as soon as possible regardless because, if they waited for SP, they'd *lose* their competitive advantage. In fact, a clearer distinction between the two types of policy would make them mutually reinforcing, providing a better focus for both governments and campaigners alike whilst helping to mobilise public support *both* for SP *and* for unilaterally implementable policies.

On the point of a presumption of a universal vantage point of rationality, whilst it may be difficult today to imagine that policies desirable for the whole world could be successfully defined, we can already see how many problems of the economy, the environment and other aspects of life are becoming truly global in scope and, furthermore, made worse by destructive global competition. As it becomes more intense, however, it is in the very nature of competition that the co-operative actions necessary to solve the problems it causes tend to become increasingly obvious. It's a bit like a competitive game a group of children might decide to make up together when there is no adult around to oversee and, if necessary, force co-operation upon them. Inevitably the children find that not all necessary rules can be defined right from the start so the game has to be tried out and further rules made up as they go along. As the game develops, and if competition risks getting out of hand, appropriate rules tend to emerge to regulate that competition – rules which can, hopefully, be agreed upon by all the children and implemented by all (simultaneously!) to avoid the game degenerating into a small war.

Indeed in the evolving game of global competitive capitalism, already today we can see proposals for policies based on global simultaneous implementation emerging; the most obvious being the Tobin Tax. Another would be U.S. Congresswoman Eleanor Holmes Norton's legislation introduced into the House of Representatives (HR-2545) calling for the abandonment of U.S. nuclear weapons *when all nuclear states do likewise.* As far as any future regulation of transnational corporations is concerned, surely it is difficult to see how any significant regulation could possibly be implemented on any basis *other* than globally and simultaneously.

In conclusion, therefore, I would say that, as global competition intensifies further, such a 'universal vantage point of rationality' *can* exist and is already beginning to emerge. As competition becomes even more acute, further simultaneous policies will inevitably continue to emerge, the proposals in this book representing but a part of that inevitable process.

It should, perhaps, also be pointed out that many of the measures of SP are likely to be characterised by their *reversal* of current destructive trends rather than by any risky imposition of untried policies that break new ground. For SP is really nothing new in the sense that, throughout human history, governments and laws have evolved in response to changes in society brought about by technical changes and other developments - what we sometimes call 'progress'. Inevitably, each new development had an impact on society on an ever larger scale. With each, new societal problems arose requiring legislation and governance to regulate and solve them, albeit imperfectly. Such regulation has also traditionally been implemented simultaneously and 'globally'; i.e. 'globally' in the sense of applying to the entire territory in question – usually a nation. The problem of international competition could be said to be merely an extension of that process of new development. But now the problems caused are *international and global*, not merely national and, furthermore, they are actually eroding the ability of nations to maintain previously attained levels of regulation/taxation and, instead, are forcing them to progressively dismantle them. As a response, SP would therefore not necessarily mean its measures would be much different in character from those implemented nationally in the past. What would mainly be new is that those 'old' policies would be implemented by all nations simultaneously. Whilst this might be rather 'unified and top-down', it would restore proper democratic governance over the world economy in contrast to what we have today which is the reverse: the world economy dictating to the world's peoples. So yes, SP is unified and somewhat 'top-down' but it is necessarily so. Nevertheless, it should also be noted that whilst its *effects* may be top-down, its *support* derives solely from individuals which is very much 'bottom-up' and democratic. Furthermore, the limited scope of SP means that it does not represent an alternative to local, small-scale initiatives but, rather, is entirely complementary to them.

As to actually defining and agreeing the SP measures themselves, it will doubtless be very difficult to do so but not, I think, impossible. So to write off the whole project in advance, as some critics would, on the assertion that 'agreement will be impossible' seems to me a rather high-handed, negative and unwarranted position to take. Surely there must be much upon which we can agree and what cannot be agreed upon, or is in doubt, can be left out.

And then, of course, there is the most common criticism of them all: "Yes, but is it *realistic?*" In posing the question of realism, however, people tend to forget that in this context it has two aspects. The first, most obvious one is whether it is realistic to expect that adoption by all nations could actually be achieved. To this, there are, perhaps, two responses. The first was given by Noam Chomsky who said of SP: "Can it work? Certainly worth a serious try." And the second is: If we don't try, we'll never find out. And anyway, if there is no better proposal on the table and disaster is looming, what do we have to lose? The second, less obvious aspect raised by the question of realism is fear. Even those who would broadly agree with the problem analysis in this book suggest that financial market re-regulation will occur first, they say, in the EU with the USA following soon after (or vice versa). Thereafter, all other nations are expected to fall into line.[1] But given the potential dangers of capital flight and the consequent fear of being the first to

---

[1] For example see *Localization - A Global Manifesto*. Colin Hines. Earthscan, 2000.

'go-it-alone', and given our undeniable human nature, is it *realistic* to expect, say, the EU to take that risk alone? After all, the leaders of the EU and their citizens might well ask: "Why should we be the first ones to stick our heads over the top of the parapet?" And indeed, why should they? So we come down to a simple fact of human nature: the fact of fear. In putting forward solutions, I believe it is fundamentally *unrealistic* to ignore that fact. To the extent that SP takes this aspect of human nature fully into account it is, I suggest, *very* realistic.

As a final comment, whilst a multiplicitous, fragmentary approach to solving problems may, under normal circumstances, be more in tune with human nature, I believe we should remember that the world does not have unlimited time in which to solve its problems. Global warming, deforestation, violent technologies and far-right political parties are not standing still. Indeed, they are already now unmistakably threatening humanity's future. In considering whether our problems require small, fragmentary solutions or a big, unified one, it may be recalled that even Schumacher, in "Small is Beautiful", himself recognised "the *duality* of the human requirement when it comes to the question of size.."; that "We need the freedom of lots and lots of small, autonomous units, and, at the same time, the orderliness of large-scale, possibly global, unity and co-ordination."[2]

How much longer, therefore, can we afford the luxury of following only a local, fragmentary approach?

ACTION STRATEGY

This book is being distributed as widely as possible amongst professionals, NGOs, individuals like you and me and any other potentially interested parties for the purpose of seeking your provisional adoption of SP. Provisional adoption by you

[2] *Small is Beautiful*. E.F. Schumacher. Abacus 1974, page 54. Italic emphasis is his.

or your organisation simply signifies your recognition of the need for certain policies to be implemented globally and simultaneously as well as your general agreement with the aims of SP. This would be a simple process, somewhat akin to a petition of signatures. (See form overleaf)

Once a significant number had provisionally adopted SP, sympathetic professional policy-makers can be called upon so that they and all of us who had provisionally adopted can come together in an open forum or conference with a view to formulating SP's definitive measures. Against a background of significant and solid support for SP, all will then have the necessary incentive to co-operate constructively in defining and agreeing its measures. Indeed, as has been suggested, since it will undoubtedly take many years to achieve worldwide adoption of SP and since we live in a changing world, the whole process of policy-making must necessarily be flexible and dynamic. It is therefore quite plausible that a series of such conferences might be held during the course of the adoption campaign so that the measures of SP can be formulated and then formally adopted, a little at a time, gradually developing into a complete set of measures by the time the adoption process was nearing completion. In this way, the whole process of policy formulation will be both flexible and completely open to all concerned.

I very much hope you will want to provisionally adopt SP. All you need to do is fill in the form overleaf and mail/fax it to ISPO. Or you can do so by e-mailing your details to ISPO at the address below. Thank you.

John Bunzl

International Simultaneous Policy Organisation (ISPO)
P.O. Box 26547, London SE3 7YT UK.

E-Mail: info@simpol.org   **Website:** www.simpol.org

"People get ready,

There's a train comin'.

Don't need no baggage,

You just get on board.

All we need is faith

To hear the diesels hummin'.

Don't need no ticket,

We'll just thank the Lord!

I believe, I believe..."[3]

---

[3] Words from "*People Get Ready*" by the late Curtis Mayfield. Mijac Music Co./Beechwood Music Ltd.

Please make a photocopy of this form – Do not tear out

I confirm my provisional adoption of the Simultaneous Policy. If, in spite of pseudo-democracy, I still have a party-political preference, I will do what I can to encourage my party to adopt SP. If I have no party-political preference, I will vote for any party that adopts it. In provisionally adopting SP, I also secure my right to participate in the democratic formulation of SP's measures:

Surname (Mr./Mrs/Miss/Ms) ....

First Name ....

Organisation *(if applicable)* ....

Address ....

....

....

....

Post Code ....

Country ....

Nationality *(if different)* ....

Telephone ....

Fax ....

E-Mail ....

Signed ....

p.t.o.

Please tick as appropriate:

□ I would be interested to send copies of the Simultaneous Policy to friends and colleagues. Please send me details on how I can order further copies.

□ I would like to become involved in campaigning for the adoption of SP.

□ I am a member of these other NGOs *(please list)*

....

□ *Optional:* I would like to make a donation to ISPO. I enclose cheque payable to ISPO in the sum of ....

□ *Optional:* I voted for *(insert party)* .... chose not to vote *(delete as applicable)* in the last parliamentary/presidential election. This election took place in

(insert country) .... on *(date)* ....

Thank you.

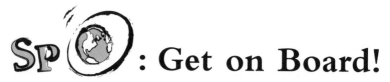

SP : Get on Board!
International Simultaneous Policy Organisation

Website: www.simpol.org
E-mail: info@simpol.org
Post: P.O. Box 26547, London SE3 7YT, UK.
Fax: +44 (0)20 8460 2035

Index